Acid Rains on Liberal Propaganda

Acid Rains on Liberal Propaganda

Ultra Liberals, Far Lefters and Global Warmers Beware

Gerald T. Westbrook

iUniverse, Inc.

New York   Lincoln   Shanghai

Acid Rains on Liberal Propaganda
Ultra Liberals, Far Lefters and Global Warmers Beware

iUniverse, Inc.

For information address:
iUniverse, Inc.
2021 Pine Lake Road, Suite 100
Lincoln, NE 68512
www.iuniverse.com

ISBN: 0-595-33419-9 (Pbk)
ISBN: 0-595-66914-X (Cloth)

Printed in the United States of America

Contents

Preface

This book is about the global warming issue and the Kyoto Treaty or Protocol. It is about environmental and energy development. It is about the 2000 and 2004 presidential elections. It is about the propaganda campaigns from all of these areas. This book, in part, is a political history covering the above two presidential elections and some of the events in between. Politicians covered include Albert Gore Jr, Tom Daschle and John Forbes Kerry.

The original title, for this book of essays, was *The Invasion of the Gorons*, an invasion by a band of creatures from the planet *Gore*, intent on dramatically increased environmental and climate regulations. This initial title was also the prefix title for seven of the incorporated essays. However, this title was dropped for a variety of reasons. The first was concern that such a title would lead to this book being stacked in the science fiction section of many book stores. Another reason was that it was not a title that would rapidly focus a potential reader on the subjects and issues involved.

A new title would need to provide better focus, but would also be a bit more prestigious and dignified. A switch was made to *Pimps, Prostitutes & Propagandists*. The *Pimps and Prostitutes* labels were meant more for those on the sidelines that, for one reason or another, choose to get involved in the political warfare. These might be commentators, writers, journalists, actors, singers and so on. Surely not all of these are pimps or prostitutes, but many are.

My family was a bit skeptical that I had met the prestigious and dignified tests, hence a third title was needed which led to *Policies, Politicians & Propagandists*. Policy development, and politicians running for election are the major activities that bring the propagandists out of the woodwork. While there are many excellent politicians, there are many that are mostly propagandists.

Still this title does not even hint at the acidic satire present in this book. A fourth title was needed, built around the central theme of propaganda, but giving some indication of the approach used. I also like the word rhetoritician, namely one who can take any subject and talk endlessly on either side. Surely, John Kerry is a master of this art. However that word is not as strong as propagandists, so the propaganda theme remains. This thinking has led to the title: *Acid Rains* on Liberal Propaganda, and the sub-title that warns this book is unsafe for liberals and global warmers.

This book is about political war, the dirty tricks involved in such war, and the propaganda vortex that any war brings. Peggy Noonan, the former speech-writer for President Reagan, commented on a TV talk show just before the 2004 election, how terrible she felt about voter fraud. She also stated, very strongly, that in her judgement, the voter fraud problem is largely a Democratic Party-driven problem.

I believe exactly the same way on the use of propaganda. While there is undoubtedly propaganda created by conservatives, it is the conviction of this writer that this is almost trivial compared to that created by the Gorons. Indeed, this book was triggered by disgust at the writings of Albert Gore Jr, which will be shown in this book to be nothing more than propaganda.

Everyday we are besieged with thousands of messages. TV is so bad. Certain movies are outrageous. And magazines are particularly egregious. Many are stuck in the face of every housewife and teenager at every check out station in the country. The magazines offer *secrets* on everything: looks, stress, sex, health, environment and so on. And you are also given a one-sided message about each new political issue. And the press provides usually unlimited, un-researched and un-skeptical support on each new issue saluted.

About the Author

Mr. Westbrook and his wife were both born in western Canada: Saskatoon and Calgary respectively. He and his wife moved to the United States in 1958. They are naturalized American citizens. Their three children were born in the USA.

The writers credentials includes an engineering degree from the University of Saskatchewan at Saskatoon and advanced degrees in engineering and economics from the University of Minnesota at Minneapolis, all with a heavy emphasis on chemistry and mathematics. The author is currently a senior associate at the Institute for Energy, Law and Enterprise at the University of Houston.

The author has worked extensively, from 1955 to 1994, in the hydrocarbon industries, first with an oil company and then, five years later, with a petrochemical company. Industrial experience has been focused, primarily, on a very broad set of energy and water related problems and issues.

On retirement Mr. Westbrook has remained active in consulting, educational service, public affairs and retailing activities. His background hence includes an industrial, educational and free enterprise perspective.

The author also has 70 plus years as a keen observer and witness to nature, agriculture, research, industry, politics and society at work in five distinct geographical/political arenas of North America: Saskatchewan, Ontario, Minnesota, Michigan and Texas. He has published dozens of papers, essays, editorials and letters on energy, environmental, climate change, and political issues.

He rejects the position that, since he worked in the above industries, he cannot protest what is going on in the environmental, regulatory and political fields. Clearly, he will be charged with having a vested interest.

Financially this is trivial, with zero shares held in the petrochemical firm, and only a hundred shares in the oil company. However he reports owning several hundred shares in another oil company, that is the greenest global oil company today.

Philosophically Mr. Westbrook acknowledges he would be much more inclined to hear out industrial companies than environmental activists would be. However he also notes that he frequently operated as a maverick within these companies, and his relationship with both companies that he worked for was not always in *sync*.

Finally, he would argue the average environmentalist—who has staked out his, or her, pathway in life on the environmental movement—has a far bigger vested interest in getting their way on environmental, climate and energy issues.

In Memoriam

Lillian Jean Westbrook

Born—November 20th 1897, Portage La Prairie, Manitoba

Died—February 5th 1998, Saskatoon, Saskatchewan

For her love, her kindness and her wisdom.
For putting up with me and my demands and priorities.
For the value she placed on education.
For her love of books,
without which I would not be the person I am today.
This book is dedicated to her memory.

Gerald T. Westbrook

Acknowledgment

Alvin Hamilton, 1912–2004. While several high school teachers were important in my growth, one teacher particularly sticks out. Hamilton, while an excellent history teacher, still spent much of the lecture period telling stories about World War II. He would then give very tough reading assignments on a wide variety of history, political issues and policy studies—oh, were some of those Canadian policy studies in the 1950's absolutely dreadful. In any event he later left teaching for the political field, won election to the Federal parliament several times and ultimately rose to become the Minister of Agriculture, probably the most popular minister in Canadian history, under the reign of John Diefenbaker and the Progressive Conservative party.

Saskatchewan, from 1944 to 1964, was very heavy into socialism, with the Cooperative Commonwealth Federation (CCF) party in control. Alvin Hamilton, more than any individual, opened my eyes to an alternative—the conservative political philosophy. This influence was sealed by a reading of the book: Atlas Shrugged, by Ayn Rand, during my early university years.

I would suspect Hamilton would have enjoyed the essays in this book, the political satire involved and the overall objective of reducing the propaganda fog that exists in elections and in policy developments.

1. Introduction

An Invasion by an Alien Culture

North America, we have a problem. *Planet Earth is under invasion. Parts of Europe have fallen. And much of our continent is under intense attack by an omni-present alien group. This alien culture seems to have come out of the wood-work, but it has been around our cities for years, setting up sleeper cells and safe houses. And the members of these cells are full of unbelievable hatred towards our culture, and our lifestyle. Indeed these aliens are out to destroy all that we once valued in this country: marriage, family, home, religion, education, flag, borders and our military.*

There is no question that these aliens have declared war against the United States that we have known and loved for years. But most Americans don't even realize this threat exists, let alone the magnitude of this threat. Of course I'm talking about the ultra Liberals, and the far Left. I'm talking about the aliens known as the Gorons (see below). I'm talking about the *Gore Wars* [1], and the *Invasion of the Gorons*[2]. I'm talking about the "useful idiots"[3] who endorsed anything and everything that the communists said or did.

But who are the Gorons you might ask. Would you believe that *the scientific definition is an alien from the planet Gore, the third planet in the Alpha Centauri system. And, by a very strange coincidence, one of the very first Americans they captured and converted was Albert Gore Jr. Over time he has actually become the Head Goron (HG). Gore is also sometimes referred to as Prince Albert.* Today, while the future of the HG, as a politician, is rather bleak, the *Goron* name lives on.

In this book the Goron name will be used as a synonym:

- for those activists/politicians who embrace simplistic science as the answer to complex problems;

- for those politicians who utilize complex science to isolate rather than to illuminate an issue;

- for those environmentalists who exploit environmental and climate issues for their own purposes;

- for those global warmers who salute *The Day After Tomorrow* and *Waterworld* as gospel; and

- for those activists who believe their cause is so righteous, or want their cause to be so righteous, that it justifies any means, including deceit, violent demonstrations, sabotage and terrorism.

America, we are at war. Most wars come complete with propaganda campaigns, and this war is surely no exception. These aliens have already gained control of most of the media, most of the educational systems and most of the entertainment outlets. As a result we live in a deep ocean of propaganda. We will need very many floodlights focused on this situation—to overcome this propaganda fog and bring visibility to the public—if we are ever to get it righted. Hence this book, which, in it's own modest way, will attempt to contribute to that objective.

The Propaganda Campaign: the Pimps and the Prostitutes

Propaganda comes in all sizes, colors and shapes, spread by the pimps and the prostitutes involved. Part of such campaigns includes news manipulation and slanted messages. Manipulation includes selection, or non-selection, of specific news items and their relative treatment: headlines, space, editing and placement.

Today all of us are besieged daily with thousands of messages—from TV ads, TV programs, tele-marketers, radio, newspapers, magazines, the Internet, political pitches, political spin—and so on. Magazines are endemic. Not only do they come in the mail or in the magazine sections of book stores, but certain types of magazines are stuck in the face of every housewife and teenager at just about every check out station in the country. The magazines offer secrets on "How to Fight Stress", secrets on how to stay thin and the "Secret Sex Move No Man Can Resist[4]." And on and on and on. This former editor of the *Ladies Home Journal*—a relatively tame magazine by check-out island standards—went on: "I know from long experience that media for women tells you endlessly about stress in your life, about the way you should look, about what should make you feel sorry for yourself, or very, very fearful about your health and the environment." If that isn't bad enough, how about the media for female teenagers, that tells them endlessly about stress in their life, about the way they should look, and about sex, sex and more sex.

"In much the same way you are given a one-sided message about politics, by always being told more government is the best solution to fix any of the problems of your life." That solution applies to every area of life, including education, medical, transportation, the environment and the global warming issue.

Without the understanding that we live in a daily propaganda tsunami, individuals will become easy marks for the industrial, commercial, environmental, educational and political shysters or pimps that are now endemic in our society. The Gorons are at work.

Most observers now believe the first sighting of Gorons occurred during the Vietnam War, where Gore served as a journalist. Not only did the HG develop an interest in journalism during this war, but also in propaganda, as is apparent as one reads his book *Earth in the Balance*[5]. See below. Today, he maintains an interest in both fields. In a commentary on the HG's efforts at Columbia University, following the 2000 election, Joseph Farah reported that "Al Gore is not teaching journalism. He is teaching propaganda[6]." This was in reference to the instructions given to his students on how to prepare a critique "on media coverage of the global warming issue."

A recent essay entitled *Gore Wars,* by a judge on the U. S. Court of Appeals for the Ninth Circuit, Judge Alex Kozinski, notes the tidal wave of doomsday predictions, starting with The Limits to Growth. This tome—authored by a group of *scientists* taking the pretentious name: the Club of Rome—which the author dismisses as "a bunch of hooey; virtually nothing the Club of Rome predicted with such alarm has come to pass[1]."

Today this tidal wave of scare stories continues. Each of these are very difficult, if not impossible, for the public to assess. "They all come swaddled in dire pronouncements from the usual suspects and carry the imprimatur of some scientific-sounding group ready to vouch that the crisis will cause as much damage to Earth as the Death Star did to planet Alderaan."

Yet with each subsequent trumped up crisis the press provides usually unlimited, usually un-researched, and almost always un-skeptical support. Serving as a shill for these movements is not journalism. It is a corruption of the profession. It is prostitution, a selling out of the values of honest journalism for the adoration of the so-called *elite*, and the hope of ultimately becoming one of these *so-called elite.*

There are so may pimps and prostitutes involved in these movements, striving to attract the uneducated, the naive and the uninitiated to their political agenda. In addition to journalists, perhaps the next most important group are entertainers: actors, singers and comics. These are the Barbra Streisands of this world. These are the Linda Ronstadts of this world. These are the ones who have, for example, fantastic vocal talents, but who have used the fame gained from such talents as a pathway into the minds of the uneducated, the naive and the uninitiated. These are the ones where you want to shout out: just "Shut Up and Sing[7]."

Inevitably politicians jump on board, making the latest crisis the centerpiece of their political pitch. This process has led to frequent, costly and in many cases, "disruptive changes in our laws that are difficult or impossible to undo[1]."

The Propagandists: the Propaganda Ministry, Goron Central Command, and the NGOs

It is my conviction that the political debates in general, and the debates over environmental and climate change issues in particular, have been essentially *kidnaped* by the Gorons. This has resulted in a covert shift in emphasis and direction towards political activity and political control as the objective. Rather than a systematic effort to prioritize and eliminate environmental problems we see efforts aimed at political domination. Rather than the development of a comprehensive climate theory, we get endless fear-mongering. The Gorons are not out for science. They have no concern about preserving the scientific method. Put very bluntly, they are out for power.

As noted above, invasions inevitably include propaganda. This writer would argue that our society is under the most intense, creative and crafty propaganda campaign ever conducted in the western world. In contrast, the campaign launched by Joseph Goebbels, over World War II, literally pales in comparison[8]. [Note: what I am doing here is stealing a technique frequently used by the liberals, namely comparing their opponents to the Nazis. The author Ann Coulter points out that "the classic liberal response to a principled conservative argument is to accuse the Republicans of planning a second Holocaust. "No matter how inured one becomes to liberal hate speech, the regularity that Republicans are compared to Nazis is still astonishing[9]." Here I get the jump on the liberals by introducing their couple to Joseph Goebbels, the Minister of Propaganda for Adolph Hitler.]

The principle propaganda thrusts frequently originate at dozens of different Non Governmental Organizations (NGOs). The reader will be more familiar with such names as the Environmental Defense [Fund] and Greenpeace and so on. And each of these NGOs, many full of neo-Luddites, press their attack forward against industry, science, energy, chemicals, world trade and free enterprise. In addition many politicians, government bureaucrats, university professors and entertainment personalities all chip in, but all primarily supported via inputs from one or more NGO. While decentralized, one gets the feeling this propaganda effort is well orchestrated, by an invisible, but all powerful central command. Read on.

A number of news reports have appeared regarding the possibility that some members of the space-alien community[10] are resorting to brain implants to help enlarge their membership. While there is no evidence of any such implant opera-tions being conducted by the Gorons, this practice cannot be ruled out, particu-larly when one considers the robot-like behavior of many of the members of this movement. Indeed this attribute has often been applied to the HG himself, which is certainly food for thought.

Perhaps this robot-like behavior is best seen when the *field solders* get their marching orders from *the Propaganda Ministry*. For example, I'm sure many of you use the word *gravitas* in your daily conversations and writings. Well not hardly! I had never heard of it, over my many years on this planet, but during a period on the 2000 election—a week, perhaps two weeks—we suddenly had a *gravitas* epidemic. Every liberal talk show host and/or guest used it. Every democratic speech contained it, as did every liberal editorial and newspaper column. The context was that George W. Bush did not have gravitas. And all of these Gorons just came up with this idea independently, exactly at the same time? Well not hardly. *Goron Central Command* was at work.

The Anointed Ones

The techniques used on the environmental and climate change issues are not unique to that field. They are applied to all of the major political issues of the 20th century. Perhaps Thomas Sowell stated it best in his *Vision of the Anointed*: "What all these highly disparate crusades have in common is their moral exal-tation of the anointed above others, who are to have their very different views nullified and superseded by the views of the anointed, imposed by the power of the government[11]." Sowell reports that several key elements are common in all such movements:

- "Assertions of a great danger to the whole society, a danger to which the masses of people are oblivious."
- "An urgent need for action to avert impending catastrophe."
- "A need for government to curtail the behavior of the many, in response to the conclusions of the few."
- "A dismissal of arguments as either uninformed, irresponsible or moti-vated by unworthy purposes."

Key examples of the *Anointed Ones* include John Kerry, Bill and Hillary Clinton and Albert Gore Jr. in the United States, Jean Chrétien in Canada and Jacques Chirac in France. Here we will limit our comments to the HG. He pro-vides a perfect illustration of the mentality of the *Anointed Ones*. In his book he contrasts the richness of nature to the emptiness of our civilization.

Certainly nature is rich, but so is much of our society. But the HG can't see that. He charges that we live in an "inauthentic world of our own making[(5)]." He observes this false world was created by people, to distract people from their psychic pain. He claims that only by awakening from such in-authenticity will the cycle of psychic pain and environmental plunder be broken. Heavy! Heavy! Heavy! It is not quite clear how the HG, who grew up in a hotel in Washington, earned credentials to decide what is authentic in life and what is not. Or who is authentic and who is not. Will we, *the non-authentic*, someday all be sent, by the *anointed ones*, to some Gulag camp to be *re-educated*.

Book Organization

There is little question that we live in a deep ocean of propaganda. We will need very many floodlights focused on this situation—to overcome this propaganda fog and bring visibility to the public—if we are ever to get it righted. Hence this book, which, in it's own modest way, will attempt to contribute to that objective. This war with the Gorons goes on and on, with no end truly in sight. But the fight must be engaged at every new offensive, if we are to avoid the Gulag.

Thirteen essays are included in this book, each focusing on some unique propaganda battle.

(1) Seven Invasion of the Gorons essays provide overviews on the particular issues involved, where they have been waged, and on how these battles have been fought. Parts of these essays were originally published at *Eco-logic Powerhouse On-line*.

- *The Invasion of the Gorons-I: The Global Warming Issue.* This essay covers Albert Gores efforts to con the public on this climate change issue.

- *The Invasion of the Gorons-II: The Florida Invasion.* This chapter recalls the Florida Campaign, where the Gorons raised the art of ballot counting to a new level.

- *The Invasion of the Gorons-III: Just Look What the Gorons Have Done to Californian Energy.* This situation included brownouts, severe financial losses, total state humiliation and a new governor.

- *The Invasion of the Gorons-IV: The Emergence and Submergence of Tom Daschle.* Daschle is Dr. No himself, and his creed is: "*Whatever It Is I'm Against It*".

- The Invasion of the Gorons-V: The Revenge of the Gorons, is a story where some EPA bureaucrats skewered the Administration on global warming.
- *The Invasion of the Gorons-VI: North of the Border.* This Canadian frontier battle featured Jean Chrétien and David Suzuki and the Kyoto Treaty.
- *The Invasion of the Gorons-VII: The Kerry Enigma.* This essay covers a bit of the history of John Forbes Kerry. The objective is a search for his true identity. Eight options are identified.

(2) Parts of one essay appeared in the *International Association for Energy Economics, News Letter.*

- *A Debate on Global Warming Science & a Surprise Conclusion on the Kyoto Protocol.* This debate involved three warmers, one neutral and three skeptics. This essay reports how this group voted on the Kyoto Protocol.

(3) Parts of one essay appeared in 2002, as a guest editorial on the web site: *Center for the Study of Carbon Dioxide and Global Change.*

- *The Hockey Stick, the Little Ice Age and the Medieval Warming Period.* Here the issue involved is the conventional wisdom on how the average Earth temperature has varied over the past 1000 or so years. The *warmers* have unilaterally swept aside the past views without any debate whatsoever, and replaced these with their own views, which has been labeled the *Hockey Stick*. The *warmers* view is, conveniently, a *perfect graph*, to make the case that our planet is warming dramatically. This essay was published just prior to the start of an incredible hissing contest on this so-called *hockey stick*. However, a detailed review of that contest will be left for a future book.

(4) Parts of two essays were originally published as a paper or letter in the *Oil & Gas Journal.*

- *The Administration Policy on Carbon Dioxide Emissions.* The Gorons charge that this was a massive flip flop. It might have been a massive administrative snafu, amplified by a little bit of internal sabotage. Check it out.
- *Emissions Trading & the Uncertainties in the Global Warming Sciences.*

(5) Two essays wrap up this treatise. One has not been published before, but has been lifted from another book under preparation.

- *The Left Will Use Absolutely Anything* is an essay where they try to pin Houston's so-called terrible air pollution problems on the then Texas governor. Sorry, not his responsibility.

The last essay has several earlier versions published in various outlets.

- *Conclusions: Why I Am a Skeptic on Global Warming.* This essay summarizes the key reasons to be skeptical on this issue.

References and Notes

(1) Kozinski, Alex, *Gore Wars*, Michigan Law Review, August, 2002, Pages 1742—1767. Judge Alex Kozinski sits on the U. S. Court of Appeals for the Ninth Circuit.

(2) The key battles with selected Gorons were originally published under the banner: *The Invasion of the Gorons*, in Eco-Logic Powerhouse On-Line.

(3) Charon, Mona, *Useful Idiots—How liberals Got it Wrong in the Cold War and Still Blame America First*, Regnery Publishing, Inc., Washington DC, 2003.

(4) Blyth, Myrna, *Spin Sisters—How the Women of the Media Sell Unhappiness and Liberalism to the Women of America*, St. Martins Press, New York, NY, March 2004.

(5) Gore, Albert, *Earth in the Balance*, Houghton Mifflin Company, New York, NY, 1992.

(6) Farah, Joseph, *Al Gore and the new journalism*, WorldNetDaily, February 28, 2001. Farah also reminds his readers of the many comparisons made between the statements of Al Gore Jr and those of Ted Kaczynski, the Unabomber, including the "now-famous Gore-Unabomber Quiz".

(7) Ingraham, Laura, *Shut Up & Sing : How Elites from Hollywood, Politics, and the UN Are Subverting America*, Regnery Publishing Inc., 2003.

(8) Reimann, Victor, *Goebbels*, Doubleday & Company, Inc., Garden City, New York, 1976.

(9) Coulter, Ann, *Slander—Liberal Lies About the American Right*, Crown Publishers, New York, NY, 2002.

(10) *The space—alien community consists of Gorons, Gluons, Muons and Morons. The Morons originated on planet More, the neighboring planet to planet Gore. Since Gorons and Morons are so much alike it is essentially impossible to tell them apart. In this paper only the Goron name will be used, but the reader should be aware that anytime the Goron name is used, it is very possible that, that Goron, might in reality be a Moron.*

(11) Sowell, Thomas, *The Vision of the Anointed*, Basic Books, A Division of Harper Collins, Inc., New York, NY, 1995.

2. The Invasion of the Gorons-I: The Global Warming Issue

Their History on Planet Earth

It is not at all clear when the first sightings of the Gorons [1] occurred. It surely was sometime after the Roswell Incident of 1947 and all of the fuss over whether UFOs exist or not. Carl Sagan has painted an incredible picture of the challenge of disproving the existence of UFOs[2]. Surely the UFO's must be real. How else could we be surrounded by so many Gorons. Note that the Head Goron (hereinafter referred to as the HG) is sometimes known as Albert Gore Jr., and sometimes even referred to as Prince Albert. The first sighting was certainly before the ultimate release of his **manifesto—*Earth in the Balance*—**in 1992. In this epic document the HG could be seen describing what must have been their means of transport to Earth. Note that the *HG frequently talks in code*. For example he is undoubtedly referring to their spacecraft when he talks, in the following quotation, of clouds…"On some nights, in high northern latitudes…you can sometimes see a strange kind of [spacecraft] high in the sky…shimmering above us with a translucent whiteness, these [spacecraft] seem quite unnatural. And they should: [these spacecraft, at the edge of space] have begun to appear more often[3a]…." Here the code word *spacecraft* has been inserted for clouds, and the words *these spacecraft, at the edge of space* have been inserted for noctilucent clouds. Well perhaps this is too free of a translation, but most observers will agree that it surely has a ring to it. In any event, the first sighting[3b] was also before their **Earthday1990 essay**, where the head Goron interviews himself on global warming. The result of this interview is that he comes out in full agreement with himself. More on this subject later. In concluding this introduction to the Gorons, most knowledgeable observers now believe the first sighting of Gorons occurred sometime during the Vietnam War, where the HG served as a journalist for the *Stars and Stripes*.

The Gorons started to execute their offensive sometime in the late 1970s after the HG was elected to the House in 1976. It perhaps is not important to pin down precisely the exact date of the first battle with the Gorons. That task can be left for future historians. More importantly, it is quite clear now what their objective was, and is, namely to infiltrate wherever possible and to ultimately control the U. S. government, then the U. N. and soon the whole world. Along the way they intend to drastically change the world into their vision. More on this shortly. The HG has made significant progress on their plan with his election to the Senate in 1984 and then to the Vice Presidency in 1992. And now this year he is going after the presidency. His record indicates he is a *policy wonk*, that is a policy-minded politician, but *with a strange streak of extremism*[4] *in him.*

Key appointments of Gorons would include: Carol Browner (one of the HG's key lieutenants while he was senator from Tennessee) to head up the EPA; Timothy Wirth (a former Colorado Senator, a former Undersecretary of State for Global Affairs and a former point man for the Clinton Administration on global warming) to head Ted Turner's new United Nations Foundation; and Eileen Clausen (a former assistant secretary of state) to the Executive Directorship of the new Pew Center on Global Climate Change.

The controversy over brain implants was noted earlier as well as the robot like behavior of many of the Gorons, including the HG himself, which is certainly food for thought.

Their Vision

What do the Gorons want? This would include, for example, dramatically increased environmental regulations, and just possibly a new Climate Protection Agency. It would also mean no new SUVs (sports utility vehicles), lots of ZEVs (zero emission vehicles), lots of bicycles, far more mass transportation and the end of *urban sprawl*. This issue of *urban sprawl* has literally come from outer space. As such it would seem to be the latest offensive of the Gorons, coming to the forefront as we approach the 2000 presidential election.

What do the Gorons believe in? Clearly the HG has become famous for his intense interest in the environment and in global warming. However some of the statements and writings by the HG are quite revealing and most disturbing—

- In this quote he equates the dangers to the environment today to the dangers of nuclear war. "Nuclear war is an apocalyptic subject, and so is global environmental destruction. [We must sound the alarm] loudly and clearly of imminent and grave danger[2, 5]."

Can this be a truly sound judgement of the state of the environment after years of the EPA, after years of automobile fuel and exhaust improvements and after billions of dollars of environmental control investments in all our utility and manufacturing industries?

- This quote broadens the doomsday view to the ecology. "Today the evidence of an ecological Kristallnacht is as clear as the sound of glass shattering in Berlin[6]."

Again can this be viewed as a precise, sound and fair diagnosis of the ecological situation?

- In this quote[2, 5] he equates Americans' use of natural resources with Nazism. "...the environmental crisis is so serious that I believe our civilization must be considered in some basic way dysfunctional.... In this terrible century...we have witnessed some especially malignant examples of dysfunctional civilization: the totalitarian societies of Nazi Germany under Hitler, fascist Italy under Mussolini...in psychological terms, our rapid and aggressive expansion into what remains of the wildness of the earth represents an effort to plunder from outside civilization what we cannot find inside."

Yes, in the HG's mind, our society's embrace of what he calls consumptionism, resembles Nazi Germany society's embrace of totalitarianism.

- In this quote he contrasts the richness of nature to the emptiness of industrial civilization. According to the HG we live in an "inauthentic world of our own making[2, 6]." Life can be easy, we assure ourselves. We need not suffer the heat or the cold; we need not sow or reap or hunt and gather. We can heal the sick, fly through the air, light up the darkness, and be entertained in our living room by orchestras and clowns whenever we like." Further into this quote he observes this false world was created by people to distract people from their psychic pain. He asserts that the world of leisure, air conditioning, industrial agriculture, modern medicine, and home entertainment is not good in itself. It is but a fleeting sideshow. Finally he claims that only by somehow awakening from such in-authenticity will the cycle of psychic pain and environmental plunder be broken.

It would seem that the HG, when dealt a lemon, would not make lemonade. It would also seem that the HG, when asked to judge if the glass was half full or half empty, would vote on the half empty side, then pontificate on how close it was to being totally empty. It is not quite clear how the HG earned credentials to decide what is authentic in life and what is not. It begs the question as to what will be done with the inauthentic people. If he were elected, would we see the building of training camps where such people could be sent to be re-educated as to what was authentic and what was not.

- Finally, two quotes provide a hint on his modus operandi, once in power. The first quote indicates that he, as head of the Gorons, has a master plan. "I honestly and sincerely believe that I know exactly what needs to be done. And I am impatient to do it[7]."

The second quote is the rather famous one: "There is no controlling legal authority." One should look at both of these as a kind of warning that the HG would run roughshod over any opposition in areas where there is any ambiguity on control. The HG seems to have come up with the following modus operandi. First he will proclaim an unprecedented environmental catastrophe is at hand. Next he will indicate only a handful of ignorant and unqualified dissenters oppose this assessment. Finally he would indicate that such dissenters are preventing him from moving ahead to solve this problem. He is reported as very impatient with half measures. The HG[5] has few gifts in the art of compromise and no discernable interests in opposing arguments. He tends to regard dissenting views as heresy and ascribes evil to antagonists. When he meets people with whom he disagrees he can be condescendingly hostile.

As noted above the HG has a strange streak of extremism[4] in his makeup. He clearly is not happy with our society. He equates environmental activists to resistance fighters[6]. But does not this group of activists include eco-saboteurs? Clearly the HG does not limit his concern to just the environment, but declares that we are in a midst of political, informational, inner-spiritual and deep philosophical crisis. It is believed that this awareness of the information crisis *led the HG to invent the Internet*. He is credited with being the sole author of his book and to have put his heart and soul into it. Surely he believes[6] in his book and all its comparisons of our society with Nazi Germany's or to the former USSR's. In spite of his sincerity all of the above quotes and comments have earned him the extremist tag.

No where has this been better exposed than in a column[8] by Tony Snow. In this essay he contrasts statements by the HG to those of the Unabomber, hereinafter referred to as the UB. Snow along with Rubman[9], from MIT, noted that the vision advocated by the UB sounds much like that stated in the HG's 1992 manifesto. The HG distrusts unbridled technology, as does the UB. The HG frets over the fate of his adopted planet and thinks people must embrace revolutionary cures. The difference between the UB and the HG is that the HG wants to achieve this via massive government bureaucracies, while the UB would achieve this through mail bombs.

Apparently when the FBI agents took control of the UB's cabin they found a copy of the HG's book, complete with extensive margin notes. Note that this book was not included in the evidence list of 80 books found in the UB's cabin. Nor was this finding reported in the main street press to any significant extent. In spite of this slack reporting and/or editing practices it would seem that the truth has come out: namely that the UB is in reality another Goron, albeit if somewhat incapacitated at the present.

Their Chart

Figure 1 is similar to the chart used by the HG in his lectures on global warming, with the exception of a single point. Several times over this decade[3a, 3b] the HG has strived to couple the Earth's average temperature with the atmospheric concentration of carbon dioxide (CO_2). As evidence he will typically show a graph of **temperature** and **atmospheric carbon dioxide concentration** plotted versus time over a span of 160 thousand years (160 KYs). It is very possible that the Gorons have more than one chart, but in listening to the HG one would conclude Figure 1 was it. The HG himself has defined the data behind this chart as **the most compelling evidence** of a correlation between carbon dioxide in the atmosphere and the atmospheric temperature. On inspection both variables exhibit a *saw-tooth* profile over the 160 KY period. The graph for each variable is of a similar shape, and appear to move somewhat in parallel, but with much volatility over this period. Based on such a chart the HG would make the following claims or statements:

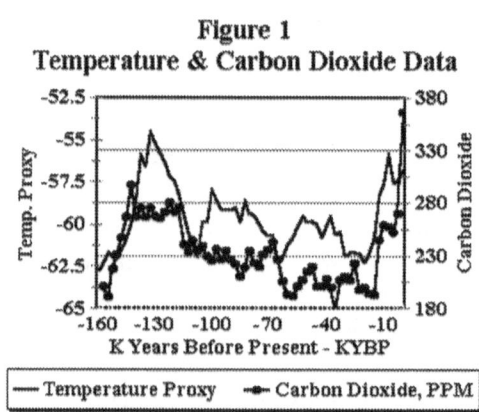

Figure 1
Temperature & Carbon Dioxide Data

- Carbon dioxide concentration and temperature have moved in **lockstep** over this period.
- Since they have moved **in tandem** over 160 KYs, it would be irresponsible to assume they will not continue to move together in the future.
- The facts portrayed here are not in dispute.

However, one must object to the use of the words lockstep and in tandem. These are far too strong for a simple visual correlation. The implication is also made that the change in CO_2 concentration precedes the change in temperature and hence is the cause for the change in temperature. However it is impossible to tell this from such a graph. Indeed one could just as easily claim the reverse correlation was proven by this chart. Yet based on this graph the HG is making what is simply a visual correlation and basing all of his conclusions on that eye-balled relationship.

One must also object to the HG's claim that the facts are not in dispute. One point on the HG's graph is not a fact, but a forecast. Note that the graph used by the HG, in his two references, is different from Figure 1. It has one point dramatically different. This is the last point for carbon dioxide, which is almost off the chart. In Figure 1, the last point shows a carbon dioxide level at 360 ppm. In contrast, the HG's manifesto shows this point at 660 ppm, about 300 parts higher. Again, this point at the 660 ppm level, is not a fact, but a forecast, or better, somewhat of a wild guess, for the year 2100. Besides being a projection and not scientific data, it really does not belong on his graph as it distorts the vertical scale to an unbelievable degree.

Finally, note that the time span of 160 KYs on Figure 1 is displayed over a space little more than two inches in width in his book. Hence **data on this graph is highly compressed.** This means, for example, that the history of 20 KYs, from the time of the Last Ice Age to the present, would be portrayed over a space of only a quarter of an inch. Further, the basic time unit for the data in Figure 1 is about 2,500 years per point. Hence a single tic on this graph—1/32nd of an inch in width—would represent the last 2,500 years of history, taking us back to 500 BC. Let me repeat that for needed emphasis: a mere 1/32nd of an inch on the HG's chart would be used to capture all the huge number of weather events over 2,500 years and to average these out to a single point.

Others have also critiqued the HG's interpretation of this data. For example, Idso[10] reported that the scientists who developed this data, from deep antarctic ice cores, had noted that:

- In a warming era (in going from cool to warm or glacial to inter-glacial conditions) changes in carbon dioxide concentration **can not be shown to precede** changes in temperature.

- In a cooling era (in going from warm to cool or inter-glacial to glacial conditions) not only does the above statement still hold, but one **can now show that temperature change always occurs first**, followed by carbon dioxide change.

After studying his record it becomes very clear that the HG "talking about science and technology is like Fidel Castro talking about freedom and democracy—each knows little about of what he speaks[9]." While the HG's "words sound good and his show may be impressive, his actions are destructive."

The forces behind temperature change

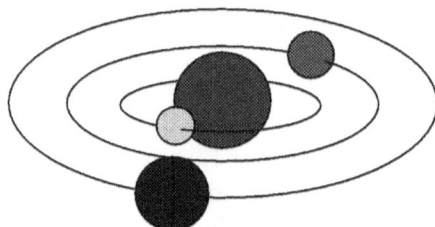

Figure 2—The Sun and 3 Inner Planets

How is it that the HG's *most compelling evidence* is so readily refuted? Idso's answer[10] was that the HG's basic premise is simply invalid: **our planets temperature is not primarily controlled by carbon dioxide.** If a change in atmospheric carbon dioxide concentration is not the cause for a change in temperature, what could be the cause? Two major sources are given as answers to this question.

(1) **Orbital Mechanics.** The answer is found, in part, in what is known as the Milankovitch Theory of the Paleoclimates[11]. Milutin Milankovitch, a Serbian astronomer/climatologist, developed this analysis from 1920 to 1941. But it was not until 1969 that it was translated to English. It has been updated and fine-tuned since then. The basic tenets of this work are that there are three attributes in the Earth's travels around the sun, that have long term impact on our climate. These attributes are:

- a 100 KY cycle in the orbital eccentricity,

- a tilt of the planet with a 41 KY cycle, and

- a wobble of the axis with 19-23 KY cycles.

While unnoticed over any individual's lifetime, these attributes—what this writer calls the Earth Motion Anomalies (EMAs)—exhibit major variation over the 160 KY period. For example the tilt of the Earth would vary over a range of about 22 to 26 degrees, with a current value of 23 degrees.

The Milankovitch theory is widely accepted as the primary force behind the climate changes shown in Figure 1, and indeed the primary cause of the Last Ice Age. The changes in the EMAs cause major variation in the solar insolation, the energy that reaches the Earth at a particular latitude and season. While carbon dioxide concentration changes are present in the historical record, more and more data lead to the conclusion they are secondary trends, not the primary cause. Indeed it is highly likely that temperature change precedes carbon dioxide concentration change.

- If the solar insolation very gradually drops, due to changes in the EMAs, then this will be followed by an equally very gradual temperature drop.

- Colder temperatures will lead to reduced carbon dioxide concentration in the atmosphere, as more carbon dioxide is taken up by the oceans.
- With colder temperatures more water will be locked up in ice fields.
- With more snow and ice cover, the average albedo of planet Earth will very gradually increase thus reflecting more energy.
- With more water molecules locked up as ice, the sea level will very slowly drop.
- The planet becomes drier. Dust aerosols increase. They have been reported to have been as much as 100 times as great as to-days level.
- There occurrence in the polar regions indicate that air circulation was also much higher than today.

These increases in the levels of natural aerosols, and the reduction in carbon dioxide concentrations will enter to play re-enforcing roles.

All of the above forces created the period known as The Last Glacial, a period all most unholy in its nature. Repeated cooling, warming and more cooling occurred from 116 to 13 KY ago, the end of the Last Ice Age.

These phenomena will impact our climate on the 100 KY and 10 KY time scales and possibly even down to the 1 KY time span. However it is unlikely they would have any impact on our climate over the annual, decadal and century time scales that are important in the current debate on global warming. They are included here to illustrate the wide span of natural climate variation and also to help clarify the interpretation of the data in Figure 1 that has been repeatedly misrepresented by the HG.

Figure 3. Both the breadth of solar output: solar irradiance, UV rays and the solar wind—and the dynamics of solar output: the 11 year sunspot cycle, other solar cycles and solar random events—contribute to our climate.

Some argue the science is done, but to claim we know all key aspects about the behavior of our sun, and other astrophysical, biophysical, geophysical and oceanographic factors is spurious, at best.

(2) **Solar and Galactic Physics.** On a much shorter time scale the answer to temperature change is also found, in part, in the behavior of our sun. The sun is the source of essentially all our energy, hence anything that changes it's behavior could affect planet Earth. Since we have seen anomalies, on or by our planet, that leads to climate cycles, we should not be surprised if other anomalous behavior exists, on or by the sun, that also can lead to other climate cycles.

It is well known that a 11 year sunspot cycle exists, which modestly affects the solar output over this cycle. Gorons have repeatedly argued that this variation in solar output is just too small to have any impact on our climate. However recent data[12] show that galactic cosmic rays, rays that bombard the Earth continuously, are modulated by this solar magnetic cycle. This increases or decreases their assistance in cloud forming activity, in counter synchronization with the solar cycle. These two processes together could be sufficient to explain most of the short term temperature variation we have seen this century.

If that is not enough it is also believed that many other solar cycles exist. For example, the 80—90 year Gleissberg cycle seems fairly clear in the sunspot record. Longer cycles are hinted at in the Sunspot record with the Spoerer Minimum around 1500 AD, the Maunder Minimum at 1645 to 1715 and the Dalton Minimum at 1795 to 1825. These Minima likely contributed to the Little Ice Age that impacted Europe dramatically from about 1300 AD to about 1850 AD. See Chapter 10.

(3) State of Climate Science

There has been major scientific progress over the past decade in all of the global warming sciences, particularly in such areas as astrophysics and oceanography. And this progress raises a major possibility that part, perhaps even all of any warming we maybe seeing is due to natural forces. Further this science also indicates there is no Armageddon just around the corner, and society has the time to pursue a more complete understanding of our climate. Science in this field is still embryonic and much more research is needed to prove out key hypothesis, adequately define process mechanisms and to reduce the many areas of high uncertainty.

In contrast the Gorons argue that the science is done and we know everything we need to know to move ahead into policies, treaties, legislation and regulation. Nothing could be further from the truth. However, one can rest assured that the Gorons will press on regardless of the facts, with the so-called Kyoto Treaty or Kyoto Protocol(KP) dominating this activity. The KP would require participants to dramatically cut their *Greenhouse Gas* emissions, primarily CO_2, which translates to fossil fuel use.

Perhaps the Gorons have a hidden agenda at work here—**the Gorons just might want to get society corralled and heading onto the reservation**—before new scientific findings rule their apocalyptic scenario invalid, and indeed, inappropriate.

Summary

Yes, the *Invasion of the Gorons* is on in full force on a multiplicity of fronts. The global warming arena is one of these. Some say this battle is already lost because the Gorons have infiltrated the media and the educational system so thoroughly. In a recent powerful, but most disturbing essay[13], James Henry talks about the strength of the ideological Left. He notes how the Right has allowed the Left to capture the media, the universities, much of the school system and the entertainment industry. He also notes that one member of the Left, Secretary of State Strobe Tolbert—who surely must be a Goron—has even announced that the end of the United States, in its current form, is near. While it may be true that much infiltration has occurred, it is not time to concede victory to the Gorons. This battle is extremely important. If the Gorons can prevail on the global warming issue, with the weakness of their scientific case, one would have to conclude they can prevail anywhere.

One of the assets, in fighting this battle, could be the Internet. This just might prove to be a way around the monopoly position held by the mainstream media on what we are allowed to read or see. It would be rather ironic to have this tool be the cause of the downfall of the Gorons with the HG as it's self proclaimed inventor.

Indeed, the Gorons may have a critical weakness—their leader. His judgement is seriously flawed by his visions of Armageddon and his agenda. His extreme statements in his manifesto and elsewhere, his rather imperious and autocratic modus operandi including little capability in the art of compromise and finally his rather simplistic views of science and technology, may all come back to haunt him. Somewhat over two hundred years ago America rejected the royal system of kings and queens. It is not too late for America to also reject Prince Albert and his fellow Gorons.

References and Notes

(1) Parts of this essay were initially published in three outlets:
   • eco-logic on-line, July 15, 2000.
   • Austin Review, August 1, 2000.
   • Citizens for a Sound Economy, August 24, 2000.

(2) Sagan, C., *The Demon Haunted World—Science as a Candle in the Dark*, Ballantine Books, March 1997.

(3a) Gore, Albert, *Earth in the Balance: Ecology and the Human Spirit*, Houhton Mifflin Company, New York, NY, 1992.

(3b) Gore Jr., Al, *To Skeptics on Global Warming...*, New York Times, April 22 1990.

(4) Terzian, P., *Bland Ambition*, The American Spectator, August 1999. This essay is based on the book—*Gore: A Political Life* by Bob Zelnick, a former ABC News correspondent. Terzian credits Zelnick's reporting as enabling him to see Gore with some clarity and to help him to penetrate the mystery of this politician.

(5) See *Environmental Scientist Dossier: Albert Gore, Jr.*, by The National Center for Public Policy Research, March 21 1996.

(6) Wolfsan, Adam, *Apocalypse Gore*, Copyright 1999, National Review, March 8 1999, as reprinted with permission on www.junkscience.com/feb99/apocgore.htm.

(7) See *Newsmakers Albert Gore Jr.*, ABCNews, 2000, quoting Vanity Fair magazine, March 1988.

(8) Snow, T., *Unabomber gore's technology*, The Detroit News, September 21 1995.

(9) Rubman, G., *Hypocrite Gore Should Practice What He Preaches*. See: www-tech.mit.edu/V116/N27/gore.27c.html, June 7 1996.

(10) Idso, S., *Carbon Dioxide Warming is Good for the Planet*, New York Times, May 7 1990.

(11) Berger, A., Introduction to the Milankovitch Theory of Climate", Review of Geophysics, 26, November 1988.

(12) Svensmark, H., and Friis-Christensen, E., *Variation of cosmic ray flux and global cloud coverage...a missing link in solar-climate relationships*, J. of Atmospheric and Solar-Terrestrial Physics, 59, 1225-1232, 1997.

(13) Henry, J., *The Left's War against America*, The New Australian, Number 137, October 11-17, 1999 as reported on www.newaus.com.au/USReport.html.

3. A Debate on Global Warming Science & a Surprising Conclusion on the Kyoto Protocol

Introduction

This debate[1] brought together seven global warming scientists—many with international reputations—and one prominent science writer to discuss the science behind global warming. This group was fairly split between skeptics, neutrals and proponents. The event drew an eclectic and heterogeneous audience of about 300, including 40 to 50 high school students and their teachers[2]. The structure of the meeting included seven presentations, lunch and two additional talks after lunch.

What follows is not a detailed review of each paper, but rather some highlights and this writer's view on the overall tone of the meeting. It was rather difficult for each scientist to make concise

Participants at the Houston Global Warming Debate	
Name	**Affiliation**
Proponents	
Dr. James Hurrell	NCAR*, Boulder
Dr. Jeffrey Keihl	NCAR, Boulder
Dr. Stephen Schneider	Professor, Environmental Biology and Global Change, Stanford U.
Neutral	
Dr. Gerald North	Distinguished Professor, Head of Climate Research Project, Texas A&M University
Skeptics	
Dr. John Christy	Earth Systems Science Lab, U. of Alabama, Huntsville. Key scientist for NASA Satellite Data Base.
Dr. David Legates	Associate Professor, S. Regional Climate Center, Louisiana State University.
Dr. Richard Lindzen	Alfred P. Sloan Professor, MIT.
Science writer	
Dr. Richard Kerr	Science Magazine

* NCAR—National Center for Atmospheric Research

and lucid presentations in the time available. What was achieved however was to see all of these individuals *in action* and to observe that a deep and complex debate on global warming exists. In the past the existence of a debate has been down-played and skeptics have frequently been depicted as few in number, negative, on the marginal side of the science and even a bit crazy. In contrast the skeptics came across as positive, brilliant, human and interesting. For example Dr. Richard Lindzen, of MIT, possibly the leading academician in the climate field and perhaps the worlds most pronounced global warming skeptic, is teaching a course this year on American musical comedy. And Dr. John Christy from NASA and the University of Alabama at Huntsville and one of the key driving forces behind the satellite based temperature data, is also a minister, a missionary in Kenya and a marathon runner. Dr Christy assured the students present that the current generation of climate scientists "will leave you lots of interesting problems to solve."

History of the Global Warming Issue

Richard Kerr, from Science Magazine, opened the meeting with a brief history of the science of global warming and some of the many uncertainties involved. He noted that atmospheric concentration of CO_2 has grown at about a half a percent per year, and is now up to 365 parts per million (ppm). This is the major greenhouse gas (GHG), with other GHGs accounting for about 40 percent of the *forcing*. Kerr noted it was very difficult to forecast changes in CO_2 concentration, and reported that these values have dropped five fold from earlier forecasts.

Over the past 130 years Kerr reported an increase in ground based temperature data as 0.5 degrees centigrade, with a range of 0.3 to 0.7 degrees. It was also noted that there are surprises and unexpected behavior in this field. One such area is the existence of non-linear factors in this field. One such area is the nature of this temperature history: a warming up to 1940; a cooling to 1970; and now additional warming up to the present.

Kerr noted that future temperature change was frequently expressed as the climate sensitivity times changes in GHG forcing. Climate sensitivity is expressed in degrees centigrade per a doubling of the GHG driving force. About 20 years ago the computer models—the so-called General Circulation Models (GCMs)—gave a warming from 1.5 to 4.5 degrees centigrade. Kerr observed we haven't improved much on this estimated range in-spite of very major changes in the computer models used.

Kerr has followed this issue for years and contributed substantially to the public's understanding. Perhaps his signature accomplishment was coining the phrase *fudge factors* for flux adjustments used in the GCMs. For example he once wrote that "climate modelers have been 'cheating' for so long it's almost become respectable[3]."

The word flux is a term used to denote an energy flow in watts per square meter. There are many such flows noted in weather and climate science and inside the GCMs. For example:

(1) the solar constant at ~342 watts/m^2 as the input from the sun at the top of the atmosphere;

(2) the greenhouse effect at ~2.7 watts/m^2.

The so-called fudge factors are/were used to prevent these models from drifting into rather unstable computations. See Chapter 7 for additional comments on these factors.

Although this meeting had separate segments on the measurement of temperature and on anthropogenic versus natural climate change, the audience might not have picked up that the global warming debate really centers on these two rather simple jobs—at least simple in concept. These tasks, namely the detection of a warming and an attribution of what is the source of that warming, need to be repeated over and over again along with the relative status of each task.

While there was no specific segment devoted to policy issues, the Kyoto Treaty—sometimes referred to as the Kyoto Protocol(KP)—had a definite influence on this debate. The KP was established in December 1997 at a UN meeting held in Kyoto, only nine months prior to this debate. It requires signatories to reduce their GHG emissions (primarily CO_2) a certain fraction below their 1990 levels. It becomes effective after 55 parties to this convention, which account for at least 55 percent of the total CO_2 emissions, have fully ratified this treaty.

Temperature and Other Weather Data

Christy effectively defended the satellite based temperature record over the past ~20 years. Several adjustments have been necessary. Media reports seem to present such changes in a fashion to convey that these finally resolve major differences with surface based weather station data, and as a result, we are left with the conventional wisdom that the world is warming. Christy was confident that the basic differences in temperature trends remain. These show the satellite data with very little, if any, temperature trend versus a positive trend for surface based data. His conclusion is also supported by balloon data measurements and a third source—night marine air temperature.

Christy also expressed concern on the recent flurry of reports, on so-called extreme climate events, as evidence of global warming. As an example of this kind of hype, he cited the reports on the extreme drought in Texas this summer. He noted while Texas was dry this summer, the worst period by far was the 1930s. In that multi-year period, drought existed all the way from Canada down to Mexico. He noted, in contrast, this year Kansas has had bumper crops.

Christy concluded that climate is changing—it always has and always will. While a fraction of that change may seem to be coupled to human activities, no one knows how much.

Anthropogenic vs Natural Climate Change—the Signal to Noise Ratio

The problem of noise in the data and the noise in the overall communications on this subject was noted. Dr. Lindzen commented that most of what the public knows about global warming does not come from the scientific community, but rather from advocacy groups such as the Union of Concerned Scientists, the Sierra Club and so on. And some people from such groups distort things.

Dr. Gerald North, from Texas A&M, noted that there are *traps and minefields* all over the detection activities, and also political pressure in doing research on this subject. He felt that long-term climate simulations can help to understand the noise in the system. He introduced the radio analogy where you have a signal and static. And that is what we have with climate research. He noted you are looking for very faint signals in a very noisy system. North argued:

- that the solar signal is not yet detectable;
- that the volcanic signal is easily detected;
- and that the greenhouse gas and aerosol signals—see Chapter 7, Note 7 for a discussion of aerosols—are detected, but each are large and are near canceling each other out, so that their strength estimates are likely inaccurate.

Is this status enough for use on policy analysis questions? North answered his own question with a "not sure—maybe can do some things".

Lindzen noted that we are talking of very very small temperature changes. He suggested that natural climate variability needs a great deal more emphasis. He discussed 3 to 4 areas of natural climate variability that the large computer models do not pick up at all or do so with insufficient details or accuracy. The El Niño is the best known example of such natural climate variability.

He reported a problem today with the testing of the computer models of the climate. He sees a circular trap. Today modelers use estimates of the natural climate variability, obtained from very long term runs of a model, to test the model. He feels this approach is "on pretty shaky grounds".

Conclusions

The eight panelists were queried on the expected anthropogenic warming over the next century, given a doubling of CO_2. Two came in at 2 °C, three came in at between 1—2 °C, two came in at 1 °C and one came in at 0.3 °C.

A second query was: would they sign the Kyoto treaty? Six of the seven scientists said no. Dr. Stephen Schneider, from Stanford voted yes. Gerald North voted no, a change from his prior position based on inputs that a fully implemented treaty would only save an estimated 0.2 °C of warming by 2100. These inputs came from a Dr. Tom Wigley of the National Center for Atmospheric Research, a noted proponent in his own right. He published[4] the results from his latest computer runs in 1998. His results seemed to have had a major impact on nearly all of the participants. He found the KP, if fully implemented by all involved nations by 2010,—a very very low probability of occurring—would reduce warming a trivial 0.07°C by 2050, and another trivial 0.13°C by 2100. These amounts are so minuscule as to be unmeasurable. This means societies are literally being asked to spend trillions, on a policy that we won't know is ever doing any good. Yes, the proponents expect societies to invest trillions on this issue without any hope of knowing if these investments are ever doing any good.

Of the several questions fielded two were of particular interest to this observer. The question was raised as to where did the money come from to conduct this research. The panelists answered, randomly, with names like EPA, DOD, NOAA and finally NASA. I kept waiting to hear the words *the American tax-payer*, but they never came.

The second question was from a student seeking guidance on what his generation should do in planning for the future. Dr. Christy suggested learn how to think, find out why people think the way they do, find out where is the data they are using coming from and what kind of agendas may be behind these sources. Another way to state this would be as an analogy to the *signal to noise ratio* discussed earlier. Students—no indeed all of us—are besieged with thousands of messages every day from TV ads, TV programs, tele-marketers, newspapers, the Internet, political pitches and spin and so on. This writer wrote a paper about 15-20 years ago on what was termed the emerging communications revolution. While correct on the issue and direction, the incredible magnitude of this revolution was totally missed as the traffic volume and message quality anticipated has been totally eclipsed. We are living in a world of very low signal to noise ratio. Hence students, to become effective, need to function like *World War II radio operators striving to filter valuable intelligence out of the daily propaganda stream.* They need to learn how to process this huge data flow, assess it, deflect most of it, filter out some of the noise, store it in the back brain cells, retrieve it as needed, and compare it to new inputs from new sources. Without this capability individuals will become easy marks for the industrial, commercial, environmental, educational and political shysters.

Finally, after the session had broken up, I asked Dr. Lindzen if I was being a bit paranoid by my concern of the modelers repeated use of the word *experiment* to describe what I would call a case study or another scenario run. I felt the use of the word *experiment* conveyed a level of scientific validity that impresses me as more propaganda rather than science. My recollection: he was in complete agreement with me.

References and Notes

(1) Parts of this report have been published at:
   - eco.logic, Number 46, Spring 1999.
   - International Association for Energy Economics, News Letter, 4th Quarter, 1999.

(2) This meeting was held in Houston on September 25, 1998. The seminar was sponsored by The Houston Forum with program support from The Gordon and Mary Cain Foundation.

(3) Kerr, Richard, *Model gets it right—without fudge factors*, Science, May 16, 1997.

(4) Wigley, T. M. L., *The Kyoto Protocol: CO_2, CH_4, and climate implications*, Geophysical Research Letters, 25, 2285-2288, July 1, 1998.

4. The Invasion of the Gorons-II: the Florida Invasion

Introduction

The objective of this report is to start a movement to retain the Goron[1, 2] name. The reason for this will be noted shortly. As I write this report, George W. Bush has just been inaugurated as our 43rd president. While this recent election may have settled the battle with the Gorons in the short term, and likely has settled the future of the Head Goron (HG), the Gorons have not gone away. And simply because the HG may retire is no reason to give up this name. It is short, crisp, too descriptive, too memory provoking and too perfect a fit to abandon. As a means to remind the readers of the utility of this name, the Florida battle will be highlighted. This should also remind the readers how determined, tenacious and even ruthless this band of aliens has been, and will continue to be.

In a prior report on this subject it was noted that the Goron invasion was on in full force on a multiplicity of fronts. While it was noted[3] that we have allowed the Left to capture the media, the universities, the public school system and the entertainment industry, it was also noted that this was no time to concede victory. The Gorons are believed to be from the nearby Alpha Centauri system, specifically the planet Gore. While it is known that there are also aliens on Earth from planet Gore's neighbor-planet More—this was not reported on in the prior report. However, one can be assured that the Morons were present on the Florida battlefield, side by side with the Gorons.

The Florida invasion began in earnest on November 8th, 2000. So very much was at stake in this battle, including the presidency and all that entails. Less obvious, but of significant importance, was the desire to avoid the conversion of the global warming issue into a long-term political control and tax collection mechanism. The Gorons surely saw additional reasons that made this battle the most critical in their history and one that they felt had to be won at any cost. Their reasons included the future definition of the Supreme Court and the possibility the Democrats could be facing a 16 year Bush family dynasty. Hence the bitter and extended campaign in Florida. The HG is the proud author of "the no controlling legal authority" philosophy. Few realized that when he stated this axiom, he was defining the Florida battlefield. Fortunately, that battle is now history and the Gorons have been declared the losers. It appears there was a controlling legal authority after all, the U. S. Supreme Court.

The Florida Theater: New Gorons Emerge

When the election was over on November 7th—and the victory in Florida went to Gore, then to Bush, then to On-hold—the Gorons moved into that state by the thousands. One report[(4)] suggested these Gorons were actually parachuted into the state, but that claim has not yet been verified. Only the HG was missing in action in Florida, retreating to security inside the Naval Observatory in Washington. Perhaps he was also searching the skies for more UFO's and the arrival of additional Gorons and Morons.

Who are these new Gorons? Before identifying some of these key aliens, the reader should recognize that, since Gorons and Morons look and act so much alike, it is possible that some of those listed below may not be Gorons, but may, indeed, be from the planet More. Let me list a few:

- David Boies, the conqueror of Microsoft, and the lead attorney for the Gorons, had a new victim in his sights—George W. Bush. Boies is articulate and crafty. He may well be the most dangerous of all Gorons. He has the look of one who has swallowed *the canary* and thoroughly enjoyed it.

- Warren Christopher, former secretary of State is now little more than a hired gunslinger. This Goron has been described by the comedian Al Franken as "half beyond reproach and half dead".

- Bill Daley was among the first onto the battlefield. He is the son of the notorious Chicago mayor, one of the most creative politicians ever, one who could bring the vote out from the dead.

- Florida Supreme Court—at least four members of this court are Gorons. More on this shortly.

- Joseph Lieberman—this Goron has some similarities to Warren Christopher. While he may not be half dead, his voice surely must be.

- Jesse Jackson—Jackson is many things to many people. This millionaire can be expected to show up anywhere he can project himself as protecting his *constituents*. In spite of his recent Clintonoid like escapade, he is still a very dangerous Goron.

- U. S. Supreme Court—two members of this court are believed to be Gorons.

The Florida Theater: The Battle of the Butterflies

The first mention of a problem with the *Butterfly Ballot* brought to mind the so called *Butterfly Diagram* associated with sunspot behavior[5]. Clearly the *Butterfly Ballot* is in the same category of complexity as that of astrophysics, magnetic fields, sun-spots and so forth. Yet despite that complexity there have been reports school children mastered this butterfly ballot rather rapidly.

The charge has been made that far too many voters cast their lot with Pat Buchanan, *clear evidence of a faulty and biased ballot design*. Consider the layout. In the ballot section for presidential votes, the hole for Bush was first, Buchanan second and Gore third. However the names were listed in two columns with Bush and Gore listed in order on the left column and Buchanan on the right, but at a level in between that of Bush and Gore. Very short, straight arrows connected each name to the proper hole in the center column of the ballot. In spite of this linear design, one cartoonist had the gall to depict this ballot as linear only for Bush and a bowl of spaghetti for Gore.

Could the outcry over this ballot stem from the possibility that many felons, homeless people, and the like, were recruited to vote for Gore? For example, there have been reports of 445 felons having voted[6] illegally in Florida. Once recruited they may have been instructed, erroneously, to "vote for the second entry." They may have done that exactly, and voted for Buchanan instead of Gore. Food for thought.

Florida: The Battle of the Ballot Recounts.

A recent, very timely and very creative limerick[7] serves to set the proper tone for this subject. Yes, the Battle of the Recounts was going to be bloody. The recounts started with the machine results. Since the election was so close, a recount was mandated. This would be based on a state-wide re-reading of the punched ballots. Early results[8] indicated that Gore might pick up 1500 or so votes, but would still lose by over 200. However the closeness of this count, along with the fact that a large number of ballots had no vote for the presidency, and hence were "rejected" by this machine recount, surely motivated the Gorons. They immediately moved in for the kill, claiming those "under-votes" were

> Recount Dracula
>
> by F. Duplantier
>
> There once was a man named Vlad
> Who was known for a habit he had:
> With some pride in his nailing,
> When he took to impaling
> No one ever would challenge his chad.

really theirs. This completely ignored the possibility that many of these ballots represented those in Florida that were unhappy with all presidential candidates, and couldn't vote for any of them. In any event this provided one of the arguments for a manual recount.

Yes, the Battle of the Recounts was going to be complex. To review all of the individual recounts would be like reviewing all of the World War II battles in the Pacific: Pearl Harbor, Corregidor, Midway, Guadalcanal, Saipan, Iwo Jima and Okinawa. They seemed to go on forever. And that surely was the case in Florida: Miami-Dade, Palm Beach, Broward and Martin counties in the deep south, Seminole county in the center and Bay, Leon and Nassau counties in the far north. Surely many of these battles would be settled in court, a cause for some concern in Florida. It came as a pleasant surprise to this writer that there were some members of the Florida judicial system that were not Gorons. It is with considerable pleasure to recognize the following judges and to salute them for their professionalism, courage and legal analysis:

- Circuit Judge N. Sanders Sauls, on December 4th, resoundingly, methodically, unmercifully rejected Gore's request that Florida's election results be overturned and a manual recount of some 14,000 Miami-Dade and Palm Beach ballots be conducted. Sauls, a registered Democrat noted that Florida law required Gore to prove that a legal basis existed for ordering any recount. Gore's team failed on this count. Sauls concluded "that there is no credible statistical evidence and no other competent substantial evidence to establish the probability of a different result[4]." Sauls also noted that Gore's contest failed because he wanted recounts only in selected, highly Democratic counties, whereas the law required him to seek a review of all ballots, in all counties in the state, that used the allegedly error prone punch card machine.

- Circuit Judge Nikki Clark, on December 8th, shot down the lawsuit by individual voters in Seminole county. She rejected the claim that Republican election supervisors fatally contaminated all absentee ballots, by adding voter ID numbers to some ballot applications. Clark, a Democrat, is regarded by her peers as fair judge with integrity. She surely proved that to be the case.

- Circuit Judge Terry Lewis, on December 8th, joined Judge Clark in rejecting a similar claim for Martin county. Lewis, also a Democrat, has also supported Secretary of State Harris's decision not to accept amended, recounted vote totals.

- Florida Supreme Court Judges Charles T. Wells, Major B. Harding and Leander J. Shaw Jr., on December 8th, opposed the Courts decision ordering a recount. In particular Chief Judge Wells stated: "I could not more strongly disagree with this decision to reverse the trial court and prolong this judicial process. I also believe that the majority's decision cannot withstand the scrutiny which will certainly immediately follow under the U. S. Constitution. "My succinct conclusion is that the majority's decision to return this case to the circuit court for a count...has no foundation in the law of Florida." However the Florida Supreme Court vote was 4 to 3 for a recount. For good liberals, like four on the Florida court, when procedural justice is inadequate something new must be invented. And these Gorons, being from outer space, came up with *cosmic justice* which allows constant refinement, and "ordered another recount—selective, standardless, seat-of-the-pants[(4)]"

The End of The Battle of the Ballot Recounts

Yes, the Battle of the Recounts was going to be long and drawn out, ultimately to be settled as the Battle of the U. S. Supreme Court.

- First, by a vote of 7 to 2, this court agreed that the Florida Supreme Court judgement was "offensive to elementary notions of equal protection[(9)]," and that there were constitutional problems with the planned recount. The seven justices included two liberals David Souter and Stephen Breyer, who in an effort to win over the swing votes of Sandra Day O'Conner and Anthony Kennedy, started to play up the equal protection issue. This worked in a sense that these swing voters did break from the Chief Justices opinion, but merely substituted the equal protection aspect as their rational against a recount.

- Next they ruled, by a vote of 5 to 4, that the Florida recount plan was so arbitrary and capricious as to be not only unfair, but also unconstitutional. While the case was remanded back to the Florida court for further proceedings, at the same time the five U. S. justices said that legal deadlines would make a constitutionally sound recount impossible.

- In addition, three of the justices—William Rehnquist, Antonin Scalia and Clarence Thomas—concluded the Florida Supreme Court had violated both the U. S. Constitution and federal law in ordering a recount.

- Ruth Bader Ginsberg and John Paul Stevens thus emerged as the only Gorons on this court. They didn't disappoint as they both skewered the decision of the majority, but to no avail. The Battle of the Ballot Recounts was over.

Conclusion

While the Gorons lost this battle in Florida, count on them to carp about the injustice of this election for the next four years. Rest assured, they will not go away, so the need continues to be on our guard like never before. Communicate with them—absolutely. Invite them into the current administration—possibly, in very selected areas. Co-operate with them on legislation—only with one's eyes very wide open. As usual, they will strive to finesse every issue.

Perhaps it was appropriate that the decisive battle with the Gorons occurred in Florida. After all this is the home of Disney World, and seldom has the world been witness to a more Mickey Mouse event than the Florida battle. Where else could one hear about hanging chads, swinging door chads, dimpled chads and even pregnant chads? It surely would be appropriate for the Epcot Center, now that this battle is history, to open a technology center on "Chads" at their campus in Orlando. However it is known that the Smithsonian has agents already in the field looking for "Chads" for it's museum. Ergo, the Epcot Center better start moving fast or the Yankees will have cornered one more precious southern resource.

While one may question if a chad should be preserved for future generations to see, there is surely something more valuable to preserve out of these so many battles—and that is the name Goron. Although the HG has made no statement that he will not be around for the 2004 election, the possibility exists that he will not be. One can expect he will strive for that nomination. However many reports have already declared his political career over. As such there have been some suggestions that *the Gorons rename their organization*. This should be discouraged. After all the name Goron is such a perfect fit for all liberals, environmentalists and the global warming crowd, that this name should be preserved. It should be used over and over as a perfect, yet simple, synonym for unlimited government, robotic policy wonks and politicians that embrace endless regulations, with a special extra regard given to international regulations.

References and Notes

(1)   Parts of this essay were first published in eco-logic on-line, January 15, 2001.

(2)   See Chapter 1 for key definition of Gorons. Clearly the word Gorons has many uses. It refers to those aliens from the planet Gore. It can also be used to define supporters of Albert Gore Jr., or as a synonym for environmentalists, for global warmers, the Left or for liberals in general.

(3)   Henry, J., *The Left's War against America*, The New Australian, Number 137, October 11-17, 1999, as reported in www.newaus.com.au/USReport.html.

(4)   Krauthammer C., *Gore's campaign lived, died by courts*, Houston Chronicle, December 15 2000.

(5)   Sunspots are a freckle like phenomenon that appear on the surface of the sun, and the Butterfly Diagram is a chart of the distribution of these sunspots over a typical 11 year Solar cycle. On this chart, the Solar latitude is the vertical axis, with the year as the horizontal axis. Sun spots, at the start of a new cycle, begin to appear at relatively high Northern and Southern Solar latitudes. However this location preference gradually shifts towards the Solar equator as the cycle plays out. A plot of this distribution gives a picture similar to the wing spread of a butterfly.

Sun-spots are believed to represent areas of localized magnetic activity on the sun. They represent one of the attributes of the sun that can be observed and measured. As such, they represent an indirect measure of the activity of our sun. Proponents, of the anthropogenic basis for global warming, frequently mention that the carbon dioxide concentration in our atmosphere has increased by about 30 % over the past century, as though that represents convincing evidence that increase is the cause for any warming. In contrast they never mention that the solar magnetic flux has undergone about a 140 % increase in the same period.

(6)   Kidwell, D., et al, *Hundreds of felons cast votes illegally*, Miami Herald, December 1-2000.

(7)   Duplantier, F., *Recount Dracula*, Eco-Logic On-Line, December 15 2000.

(8)   Van Natta, Jr., D., *Democrats Tell of Problems At the Polls Across Florida*, New York Times, November 10 2000.

(9)   Gigot, P., *Liberals Discover The Tyranny Of the Courts*, The Wall Street Journal, December 15 2000.

5. The Invasion of the Gorons-III: Just look what they've Done to California Energy

Their Presence in California

Most knowledgeable observers believe the first sighting of Gorons [1, 2] occurred sometime during the Vietnam War, where Albert Gore Jr. was discovered. The Gorons were only a small percentage of the forces in Vietnam, and some of these aliens made it back to California at the completion of that odyssey. California was a perfect setting for these aliens. And have they been successful. While the invasion of the Gorons is still underway over most of America, it was close to being all over in California. Complete victory was in sight. This, perhaps, has now changed, with the emergence of the energy crisis, and the new governor, Arnold Schwartsnegger.

Several key Gorons have already been identified. Such Californians as Barbara Boxer, Diane Feinstein, Jane Fonda, Tom Hayden, Maxine Waters and Henry Waxman would all appear to be Gorons. Many others in the entertainment community, such as Robert Redford and Barbra Streisand, could be added to that list. It would certainly appear that the current California governor, Gray Davis, his attorney general—Bill Lochyer and the ex governor Jerry Brown could also be added to that illustrious set. In contrast the state Controller, Kathleen Connell, a democrat, would not make this list. Indeed, she needs to be saluted for her courage and wisdom in repeatedly standing up to the governor.

While many of the Morons that came to Earth settled in Florida, some also picked California as their home, and clearly have been as active there as they have been in Florida. The former governor, Pete Wilson, is probably not a Goron. However, since he signed off on the ignominious California electric utility deregulation plan—which we will talk about shortly—one must suspect that he very well could have come from the planet More.

The Gorons have created havoc in many areas of California. Indeed, there are charges[4] that California has been turned into a socialist state. However this essay will be limited to what they have done to the electric power system. The objective of this essay is very simple and that is depict the terrible situation the Gorons have placed the beautiful state of California in.

The Electric Power Crisis

Table 1. CA Electrical Generation Resources

Item	Capacity GW	%
Fossil Fuel Based	28.9	54
Hydro	14.1	27
Alternative Energy	5.9	11
Nuclear	4.3	8
Total Generation	53.2	100
Imports	4 - 11	-
Total Capability	57 - 64	-

California has seen many serious problems over it's history, but their current energy crisis just might be the biggest one the state has ever faced. The effects of many years of mind-boggling bumbling—by consumer, energy and environmental activists, most of whom would be Gorons; by many state politicians, and state energy bureaucrats, many of whom would be Gorons; and finally by some who populate the major energy vendors and state utilities, at least a few of which would be Gorons—started to become visible last year.

Over the past ten years California has encouraged population growth. For years California has been the place to be, whether one was a newly arrived immigrant, legal or otherwise, or the most sophisticated computer whiz, and the population has soared. California has also encouraged growth in the technology sector and other industries. A recent report from the CPUC noted: "the

Table 2. CA Electrical Plants - Age Distribution

Capacity	Age, Years	Capacity GW	%
Units of	0 - 10	4.0	7
	10 -20	14.0	26
	20 - 30	6.1	12
	30 plus	29.1	55
System		53.2	100

amount of information on the internet has increased ten fold over the past three years…Internet use by individuals in 1999 was 80 % higher than the previous year. This market has tremendous potential for growth…California simply must keep up with the energy needs of high technology, a highly productive, fast growing segment of California's economy[5]." Since 1996, the state's economy has expanded by 32 %. These two trends, along with other factors, have led to a steady growth in demand for electricity. Since the signing of their deregulation bill, in 1996, demand for electrical energy has grown by 24%.

In contrast California has discouraged the growth in electrical supply, specifically from large, central, fossil fuel and nuclear based power plants. This has been accomplished via environmental, siting and other regulatory burdens, making California the most difficult place in the world to build a major power plant. The California electrical system resources are shown in Table 1.

In addition to the *imported* electricity listed above, roughly 84 % of natural gas, the dominant fossil fuel, is imported from other states or Canada.

There is another factor about the electrical generation capability in California that is key, and that is the age of the facilities, as noted in Table 2. These numbers do not bode well for this state, either for the immediate crisis, or for it's long term health.

One might ask about recent expansions. From 1996 to 1999 only 672 MWs of capacity were added as noted in Table 3. This amount, listed, represents little more than a one percent increase from 1996 to 1999, with 70 % of this increase coming in 1996. In contrast peak demand has grown by about 12 %, and energy consumption by 24 %. It is true that significant new capacity is scheduled to come on-line this year. However, a major energy consulting firm[6] has indicated it could be 2003 before California's capacity margin could be viewed as satisfactory.

Sooner or later the above two trends were bound to interact with disastrous consequences for the state. This occurred, starting in the second quarter of 2000.

While there were some harbingers of the crisis in 1998 and 1999, it finally hit in 2000. A serious and steady price escalation started in April. Wholesale rates doubled, then doubled again in the third quarter and almost doubled again by the end of the year. Periodic and serious price spikes occurred several times, sending the California market into panic. Next the state was hit by a series of rolling blackouts. Then the generating companies tried to back away from some customers for lack of payment. Some Qualified Facilities—more on these shortly—shut down also due to lack of payment. Needless to say the credit worthiness of the state electric utilities was destroyed, and one utility filed for bankruptcy. Next the state started to buy power for the utilities, borrowing billions from the general fund; arranging for bridge loans of $4 billion, then another $5 billion; and ultimately arranging to issue new bonds on the order of $13 billion. "As a result of this energy crisis the bonded indebtedness of the state, will grow by 80% to deal with a problem that didn't exist even a year ago and would not exist now were it not for the early political decision against rate increases[7]." The state now not only has an energy crisis, but also a financial crisis, with the credit worthiness of the state starting to crumble, and the terms and conditions of future loans starting to stiffen.

Many now believe that deregulation of the electric industry was the cause for this crisis, and view energy deregulation as a massive failure. What they ignore is the California plan just might be the dumbest deregulation plan ever conceived. The founders of this great state must all be turning over in their graves at the humiliation their state is now going through.

The Causes—NIMBY and AE

It is hard to pin down exactly when the seeds of NIMBYism were sown. It probably goes back to the 60's and 70's. That was the time of the Vietnam war, and later the Three Mile Island incident. This period saw the practice of the organized protest honed to a fine edge, including the widespread use of *street theater* to make one's points. Somewhere during this period NIMBYism emerged, and spread across the country. But it rapidly grew into an epidemic in California. The reader should be aware that there are at least two other closely related diseases that hit California at the same time, namely BANANA and NOPE. These diseased attitudes have not only been focused on nuclear plants, but also on coal fired stations, electric transmission lines, off-shore oil wells, and natural gas pipelines. What the Gorons neglected to tell their faithful followers is that those who play around close to these pseudo diseases, are inevitably going to come down with a very severe attack of BOHICA, which is what is going on in California today.

With an embracement of these diseased attitudes, no major power plants have been built in California for about 15 years, and one, the Rancho Seco nuclear plant, has been closed down, after only ten years of service. And the overall energy infrastructure has been almost totally ignored. What has been built in California instead is thousands of Alternative Energy (AE) units[8]. As an example of the juvenile infatuation with AE recall what Massachusetts Senator John Kerry, a Goron from the North East, had to say last year about their Democratic convention: "The Democrats are going to walk the talk in 2000 with a convention powered on 100 percent clean energy. A clean-energy convention perfectly reflects our agenda to protect the environment, to create high-paying jobs, and to lessen our dependence on imported oil[9]." One can wonder how many high paid jobs will now, not be created, but will be lost due to this disaster. Well, the Democrats maybe able to manage the electric supply for a convention, but they have proven conclusively they can't do it for a state the size of California.

While there is no argument with the proposition that AE can be very useful, and save energy resources, it is the total reliance on AE that is one of the major reasons for the current predicament. For example California has built about 15,000 wind mills in this time period. Surely these contribute to it's electrical supply. However the amount is small, about 1¼ % of total state generation. Further, since this energy is

Table 3. Comparison between Capacity Change and Peak Demand Growth

Year	Net Capacity Change - MWs	Growth in peak demand - MWs
1996	462	2376
1997	153	2005
1998	6	2464
1999	51	(1323)
Total	672	5522

available only about 18 % of the time, additional power generation capacity is still needed to back up this source, or the over all reliability of the system would be compromised.

And this is what California has built by embracing NIMBYism and AE: a compromised electrical power system. In industry, one of the key responsibilities of the head energy executive is supply security. Clearly there is no energy supply security in California today.

The Causes—The Federal Government

There are undoubtedly several areas that the Federal Government played some role in this crisis. This essay will limits it's comments to PURPA[10]. Near the end of the 1970's the then President Carter brought out his national energy plan. This included several major laws, including PURPA. The structure[11] of the Electric Utility industry began to change with the passage of this law. This act, among it's many provisions required utilities to buy electric power from AE qualified facilities (QF's). This included wind, solar, geothermal, biomass and co-generation plants. This law was aimed at encouraging AE. Today QFs provide roughly 25 % of California's electricity.

The price for this AE would be at the avoided cost of power—the cost the utility would have normally incurred in the absence of purchases from the QF. At times the QF's could lock in their sales price for power based on oil generation. This meant the utilities would have to buy power at prices higher than they could make for themselves. One utility, SCE, has been quoted [12] as having paid $24 billion more for power, since 1985, because of PURPA.

In February 1995 FERC ended this process, stating that California could no longer require it's utilities to enter into long term contracts with AE producers.

The Causes—The deregulation bandwagon

By the early 1990's, with utilities forced to buy significant amounts of AE, power costs in California became amongst the highest in the nation at 50% above the national average. Politicians, concerned about this fact, embraced the idea of deregulation, as a means to drive down these high prices. They had visions of saving rate payers $10 billion a year from aggressive competition for this business. Hence these politicians viewed deregulation as the pathway to popularity. They were all for it as long as they could claim the credit.

Utilities were initially concerned on this movement, but came on board when provisions were made to grant allowances to these companies to recover their so-called stranded costs. These costs included investments in nuclear plants, plus the obligation these companies faced from relatively expensive long term contracts for purchased AE. The utilities believed that the provisions included enough allowances in the planned retail rates to recover these stranded costs.

The Causes—The deregulation plan

As noted earlier the California plan just might be the dumbest deregulation plan ever conceived. The key features of this plan included:

- Retail sales by the state electric utilities at fixed retail prices, set by the CPUC, an organization committed to provide low cost electricity to the people. Hence this plan should not be confused with deregulation.

- The establishment of a centralized power pool (California Power Exchange—CPEX) that would buy most of the power for the state—sometimes on contract, but far too much at market prices e.g. at prices that could float. The Gorons were certain that with deregulation, the spot price for power would crater. And they bet the future of their state on their convictions.

In 1999 there were over 400 power marketers nationally that were trading power, that is buying and selling mwhs. Perhaps as many as 300 of these were active in California. The CPEX would be located in Alhambra. This exchange ceased trading, at the end of January, 2001.

- All state utilities were required to get any and all of their power purchases from CPEX. As such they would not be allowed to enter into any long term contracts, or be able to hedge their energy situation in anyway. Again, so much for deregulation.

- A provision was included that allowed individual power customers to contract directly from generators. However the law required such a customer to pay a severance fee to it's existing public utility to permit a new supplier to service it's needs. This clause would surely discourage customers and new vendors from getting together and hence discourage new generators from coming into this market.

- Deregulation also included the establishment of an Independent Systems Operator (ISO) with the responsibility of keeping the power grid whole. As such the ISO could also make last minute power purchases, undoubtedly at spot market prices, e.g. at prices that could float. The ISO would be located in Folsom. Hence the state utilities were essentially agreeing to a pathway that would end up with a fixed price on their retail side, but a floating price on their wholesale side, a formula that ultimately made the issue of stranded cost recovery somewhat of an oxymoron.

The California Gorons, who conceived this system, were so blinded by the bonanza they thought they saw, they completely ignored warnings that their system design was seriously inadequate at best and possibly unstable at worst. One report[13] on this subject listed a half a dozen major warnings from such knowledgeable observers as the NYMEX, one of the state's major utilities— SDG&E, the California Municipal Utilities Association, at least one executive of the state CPUC, some of the energy vendors, and finally a prominent industrial consumer's group representative. Some of these concerns were later tabled, or withdrawn, probably due to pressure from state officials, and the law (AB-1890) was approved by then Governor Wilson on September 23rd, 1996.

And this is what California has built by becoming blinded by the deregulation potential, and ignoring red flags that their plan was seriously flawed: a vulnerable electrical system.

The Implementation

Part of the deregulation scheme included the divestiture by the state utilities of at least half of their non-hydro generating capacity in order to help create competition and the *free market*. Both PG&E and SCE were delighted with the prospects and went after plant sales with great enthusiasm. PG&E sold their assets for $1.5 billion versus a book value of $981 million. In turn SCE sold their plants for $1.2 billion versus their book value of $677 million. While these looked like attractive deals at the time, I suspect these utilities would surely like to have those assets back today. Further the buyers of these relatively old plants, having allocated their capital to these purchases, repairs and upgrading, and knowing of the ordeal any builder of a new plant would face, did not add any new capacity.

On March 31st, 1998 California's new *deregulated market* opened for business. The system worked superbly, and ISO officials celebrated with a lightbulb shaped cake. Brochures were available at this party that were entitled "Securing Reliability[13]." Lord, forgive these Gorons, as they knew not what they were doing. It would be three months before the party ended.

On July 9, 1998, the price for reserve power was running at around $1/mwh. Then suddenly it spiked up to $5000/mwh, where it stayed there for three hours! Then it dropped back to the $1/mwh level. Four days later it shot up to $9999/mwh for four hours. The NYMEX executive, that had earlier warned state officials, said these spikes were signs of someone probing the system, looking for the weak link.

Over 1999 wholesale prices were fairly stable. However, they did escalate from $20/mwh in the first quarter to double that rate by the fourth quarter. And for a few days in October and November prices exceeded $70/mwh.

For the first quarter in 2000 prices were back down to about $30/mwh. However, prices moved up dramatically over the next three quarters: $70, $135, and finally $230/mwh. In particular, over the second half of the year, daily average prices exceeded $150/mwh for 38 days. For four of these days, prices exceeded $600/mwh.

In industry, one of the key responsibilities of the head energy executive is price security. Clearly there is no energy price security in California today.

The Spin

Ever since this situation emerged Governor Gray Davis has sought to deflect any guilt from his office. From time to time he has flared out at President Bush, then onto FERC, then onto some state unit, or even BPA or BC Hydro. However his favorite targets have been and will continue to be Texas in general and various energy companies in particular that are headquartered in that state. These have included Dynergy, Enron and Reliant Energy. The actions have included the standard demagoguery, the hiring[14] of two ex Clinton/Gore operatives (Chris Lehane, Mark Fabiani) to escalate and intensify the attacks, repeated threats power plants will be confiscated, repeated threats of law suits, at least one pie in the face and finally the implied threat[15]—by the head legal authority of the state, Bill Lockyer—of homosexual rape of the Chairman of the Board of Enron Corporation.

While initially one might write this activity all off as the antics of Governor Gray Davis, who once held presidential aspirations, but who was now drowning. But a strategy seems to be emerging:

- we will use absolutely every resource of the state to get our way. If we can't win under the existing rules, we will use every resource of the state to get the rules changed to our liking,
- we will not only expect to win, but to come up with the blame firmly tagged on to someone else, and
- we will so discredit deregulation, that victory in the blame game will also put us in an unbeatable position on re-regulation.

At the time of writing of this report it is not at all clear whether this strategy will work and who the winner will be. The only thing certain is that we can expect a long period of many, many legal battles.

The Solution

If one could set politics aside, the road to resolution is pretty clear. This pathway[16] was, perhaps, best laid out by 31 knowledgeable individuals in academia, government and private life. Their action list included: an increase in retail prices, on at least the volume of electricity the utilities do not self supply; a commitment to the recovery of a sufficient portion of their accumulated debt to allow their return to the credit market; and completion of the necessary oversight analysis to identify any needed market reforms and a resolution, in a fair way, of the allegations of market abuse.

On the avoid list: don't make quick and irreversible commitments such as trying to isolate California from the western electrical market, don't turn the state into the permanent purchasing authority, don't spend taxpayer funds on large energy related projects; don't over commit on long term power contracts; and don't nationalize the state's electrical system.

Many economists agree that the situation would resolve itself very rapidly if California would simply embrace retail price deregulation including absolute price visibility. The price signals must get through. But how does one embrace retail price deregulation, in a state that has been brain-washed by the socialistic power structure for the past ten years. How does one gain agreement where the Governor is intent to continue to plead innocent, at the same time as he skewers everyone else, especially what he calls Texas price gougers? How does one gain agreement between parties that are as far apart as any political gap has ever been? How does one gain agreement where the far left of the political spectrum can't accept any sort of a Republican victory at best, and would rather see anarchy rule at worst? How does one put Humpty Dumpty[17] together again? It is surely not clear, at the time of writing this essay, that Humpty Dumpty can and will be put back together.

The sixth largest economy in the world is now, essentially, a socialistic government. This must be changed before California can recover from their current crisis. Until very recently the odds that this could happen were very close to absolute zero. With the emergence of this energy crisis this might just have changed. An analogous change[18], has happened recently up north in British Columbia, a governmental entity with much in common with California. Could this be a harbinger of things to come in California?

If this does not happen, if the Gorons remain in power, their victory, will be rather pyrrhic, for they undoubtedly will lead California down the pathway to becoming a *third world nation*.

Summary

Yes, the *Invasion of the Gorons* has almost succeeded in California. But perhaps they have over-stepped in their effort to create a socialistic energy dreamland. The crisis in California "is the direct result of leaders and citizens who believe they can legislate and regulate economic reality out of existence and who appear ready to stick to their fantasy until the lights go out and the economy crumbles[4]." Note it has not been the concept of deregulation of the electric utility industry that has been the problem, but rather the very unique and specific system propagated by the various Californian interests listed above. This is what California has built by embracing NIMBYism, AE, socialism, and an unshakable conviction in California's ability to finesse every situation: an energy system that is severely compromised, with no supply security; an energy system that is highly unstable with no price security and finally a financial system that is surely tarnished, including a major reduction in the overall credit worthiness of the state.

References and Notes

(1) Parts of this essay were published initially in eco-logic on-line, July 1, 2001.

(2) The word Gorons has many uses as noted in earlier chapters. In short this name has come to be used to describe any fuzzy thinker or *feel-gooder* in California or elsewhere.

(3) Not assigned

(4) For example of a report on socialism in California see the work by "A Conservative News Forum", Let's Laugh at California—They Deserve It. See: www.freerepublic.com/forum/a3ac14c4b2f25.htm, March 27 2001. (Author's comment: I would have preferred a title such as *Let's Laugh at the Gorons in California—They Deserve It*).
This report noted that "California is——a failure of socialism. It is the direct result of leaders and citizens who believe they can legislate and regulate economic reality out of existence and who appear ready to stick to their fantasy until the lights go out and the economy crumbles". This report further noted "by regulating through ideology rather than according to economic reality the government of California has effectively bankrupted the utilities and is in the process of seizing their assets. This will change the role of government from that of regulator to that of owner and operator of the states electrical grid. The People's power company. How Soviet".

(5) Kahn, M., Lynch, L., *California's Electricity Options and Challenges Report to Governor Gray Davis*, CPUC, 2000.

(6) CERA.com *North America Energy Markets in Turmoil*. See excepts from CERA's North America Electric Power Private Report, www20.cera.com/prices/research/0,1575,00.html. (Note—date is unspecified, but adjacent items show date of April 2001).

(7) Flannigan, J., *Californian's Will Be Paying Energy Crisis Bill for Years*. See: www.latimes,com/business/reports/power/lat_costs010329.htm, March 29, 2001.

(8) AE—Alternative Energy systems in California include geothermal, photovoltaic, other solar, waste energy, wind turbines and bio mass fired power plants.

(9) Kelly, P., *Head off train wreck on electricity*, Houston Chronicle, August 20, 2000.

(10) PURPA—Public Utility Regulatory Policy Act of 1978.

(11) Jurewitz, J., *Evolving Structural Change and Business Strategies in the U. S. Electricity Industry*.
See: http://econ.claremontmckenna.edu/papers/2000-34.pdf.

(12) Shoaf, R., CNN Message Board/Power Crisis, #3497, May 5, 2001.

(13) Stanton, S., *Special Report: How Californians got burned—The state electrical system is in a shambles, and the worst may be ahead. How did things get to this point?*, The Sacramento Bee News, May 6, 2001.

(14) Bay A., Are Californians Stupid, GOPUSA.com, May 23, 2001.

(15) Emshwiller, J., California Blame Game Yields No Score. Probes Reveal Little Evidence Suppliers Acted Illegally, The Wall Street Journal, May 22, 2001.

(16) *Manifesto on the California Electricity Crisis*, Convened under the auspices of the Institute of Management, Innovation and Organization, University of Califonia, 1-26-01.
See: www.haas.berkeley.edu/news/california_electricity_crisis.html

(17) For the analogy to Humpty Dumpty see Crow, B., *The Crow Capsule Summary of How California is Becoming Like India*, downloaded February 7, 2001. See: www.nabe.com/publib/caenergy.htm.

(18) Melloan, G., The Socialist Left Loses Out in Canada and Italy, The Wall Street Journal, May 22, 2001.

6. The Administration Policy on Carbon Dioxide Emissions

Shortly after his inauguration, in 2001, there was a chorus of charges that President Bush is guilty of a massive flip flop on carbon dioxide emissions[1]. An example of the buildup towards these charges was a NY Times editorial[2], citing recent evidence of global warming. It noted the President would soon have to become active on the Kyoto Protocol. It defended the KP, and argued that the KP actually favored the U. S. as it supported such things as emissions trading. Emissions trading is reviewed briefly in Chapter 7. This NY Times editorial noted that George Bush had supported the idea of regulating CO_2 in his election campaign. It concluded that this was the type of issue that needed presidential leadership, but so far he has not even made a start.

However a careful reading of the appropriate campaign speech indicates that the then Governor Bush did not quite promise to reduce these emissions. The key statement in his September 29th 2000 speech was: "...with the help of congress, environmental groups and industry we will require all power plants to meet clean air standards in order to reduce emissions of sulfur dioxide, nitrogen oxide, mercury and carbon dioxide within a reasonable period of time[3]." An analysis of this rather convoluted statement is noted in the nearby box.

Perhaps a more intimate and painful event than the NY Times editorial, was the public declaration by his head of the EPA, Ms. Whitman. For example, at a G8 environmental ministers meeting in Trieste, she reported that "the President has said that global climate change is the greatest environmental challenge that we face and we must recognize that and take steps to move forward[4]." One might wonder if Ms. Whitman had taken a lonely clause in a campaign speech, along with other inputs from the campaign, and unilaterally converted these into what sounded like official government policy. Likewise, his treasury secretary, Paul O'Neill was making news, in his own way, with his support of the KP.

> ### Governor Bush's Energy policy Speech—Key Statement on Climate Change, with interpretation.
>
> **Statement:** "…with the help of congress, environmental groups and industry we will require all power plants to meet clean air standards in order to reduce emissions of sulfur dioxide, nitrogen oxide, mercury and carbon dioxide within a reasonable period of time."
>
> **Critical Clause:** in order to reduce emissions of sulfur dioxide, nitrogen oxide, mercury and carbon dioxide within a reasonable period of time
>
> **Interpretation of the above clause:**
>
> - it is redundant in the sense that to meet clean air standards, emissions will be reduced. Note that the sentence reads perfectly well if it were omitted;
>
> - it is erroneous in the sense that carbon dioxide, not being a pollutant, is not included in the Clean Air Act and should not have been included in this list;
>
> - it states the reason we want to meet clean air standards is to reduce emissions. Hardly. Rather the reasons are to improve health and visibility. Reduction of emissions is the pathway;
>
> - and finally this clause mis-directs the attention of the listener/reader away from what I believe was the key input in this policy statement, and that was the word "all", implying a commitment to include those plants that are now grand-fathered.

Because of such activity several senators, particularly Chuck Hagel of Nebraska, contacted the White House, seeking clarification of their position on global warming in general, and the KP in particular. The answer came in a letter[5] to Hagel et al, on March 13th, which was also made public. Here President Bush confirmed his strong opposition to the KP, and that his multi-pollutant strategy would cut emissions of sulfur dioxide, nitrous oxides and mercury, but not CO_2, which, he now noted, is not a pollutant under the Clean Air Act.

At this point the chorus of charges of a flip flop reached a crescendo. The Gorons argued he should keep his campaign promise to reduce carbon dioxide emissions. These screams of indignation came from every Goron in the country.

The controversial statement was incorporated into a speech[3] presented at Saginaw, Michigan. It was an energy policy speech, entitled "A Comprehensive National Energy Policy." This was not a speech on environmental policy. It was not a speech on global warming policy. It was a speech on energy policy. However the noted statement was included at the very end of the speech and it had been assumed to be the official position of the Administration on requiring reductions in carbon dioxide emissions. At least one industrial observer commented that this was a mistake. It asked the question if campaign officials meant carbon monoxide? CO fits more logically than CO_2 on a list of major air pollutants, and is monitored and regulated by the EPA. CO_2 is not. By letting

CO_2 appear on its energy policy's list of "major pollutants," the Bush campaign was either:

- guilty of extreme administrative sloppiness, or
- had come up with a rather ill-conceived environmental strategy, or
- was a victim of internal sabotage.

This journal predicted that "we haven't heard the last of this issue[6]."

It would seem[7] that due to the intensity of the 2000 election campaign this implied commitment to reduce CO_2 emissions was temporarily forgotten. But now it was front page news. What should the President do "if he has been backed into a corner because of a single sentence in a campaign policy document and ill-considered statements from two key members of his administration[8]?" He argued this position was required now due to gas price spikes and the California energy situation. The time has arrived for setting a better course for balancing environmental and energy concerns. Christine Whitman echoed this position. "She said Bush had grown worried that restrictions on emissions would create more energy problems similar to those in California[9]." Surely regulations on CO_2 emissions would increase use of natural gas. The price for this fuel has more than doubled in the past year, a key factor in California's electricity shortages.

It is the opinion of this writer that we probably have a case of extreme administrative sloppiness here, with perhaps a bit of internal sabotage. The careful reader will note that the commitment Governor Bush made was to require all power plants to meet clean air standards. Due perhaps to sloppy staff work or poor speech writing or lack of editing, this part of his energy policy statement is admittedly a bit confusing.

Indeed, in watching TV replays of this speech, candidate Bush stumbled a bit, saying "carbon monoxide...dioxide". He appeared to be a bit startled by what was in this line. One report claimed he asked an advisor after the speech: "What was that CO_2 line[7]?" Other commentators have even suggested this line was inserted at the very last minute.

In short the controversial clause was a disaster. The speech would have been far better off without it. And the speech writer should have been given the day off after this effort.

References and Notes

(1) Part of this essay was first published as a letter to the Oil and Gas Journal, April 16, 2001.

(2) Editorial, *A Global Warning to Mr. Bush*, New York Times, February 26, 2001.

(3) See www.georgewbush.com/News.asp?FormMode=SP. See Speech Archives, use the drop down menu, select the September 29, 2000 speech, entitled: *A Comprehensive National Energy Policy*.

(4) *Climate talks secure U. S. support*, CNN, March 5, 2001. See: www.cnn.com.

(5) The White House, Office of the Press Secretary, *Text of a letter from the President to Senators Hagel, Helms, Craig, and Roberts*, March 13, 2001.

(6) Editorial, *A Bush misstep on CO_2*, Oil & Gas Journal, October 16, 2000.

(7) Hall, Mimi, *CO_2 puts heat on Bush*, USA Today, March 16, 2001.

(8) Chilton, Kenneth W., *Bush's reversal on CO_2 took courage*, Houston Chronicle, March 18, 2001.

(9) *Whitman defends Bush on emissions policy*, CNN, March 17, 2001. See: www.cnn.com.

7. Emissions Trading & the Uncertainties in Global Warming Sciences

Critique of a paper on emissions trading

This section, is a critique[1] of a paper[2] on emissions trading. This paper on emissions trading was bothersome for at least four reasons.

First that paper hit a sore spot with this writer as the authors went into great detail to calculate relative Carbon Dioxide equivalent (CO_2e) contributions— to four significant digits—for several crude oils and natural gases. For example they showed values:

- for Brent North Sea crude of 3.350 metric tons of CO_2e per cubic meter[3] of transport fuel used,
- and for Venezuela very heavy, partially upgraded crude of 4.018.

Their efforts conveyed a level of precision on the trading of energy commodities, that the uncertainties involved in global warming analysis surely would not support. Values of 3.4 and 4.0 would have been quite adequate, thank you very much. Their efforts at conveying such a level of precision, inadvertently, help grant legitimacy to the global warming issue.

Next the authors seem to believe that the arguments on the global warming issue are over and that the *politicians are in control and will set the agenda*. In the absence of a serious, considered and tenacious debate on this issue, the politicians will indeed set the agenda. And if we are not very careful they will do this from a terribly weak scientific base resulting in a nightmare set of regulations that will not solve[4] the so-called problem.

Thirdly, the authors claim they *take no sides on the climate change debate*. Yet the devotion of so much effort to write a detailed and meticulous treatise on emissions trading inadvertently gives credibility to the Kyoto program that an ever growing number of observers believe is fundamentally unsound[4]. Others have done the same thing on the concept of awarding emission credits for early investments, for example, on alternative energy systems, prior to any treaty ratification. These activities have a negative potential in that once an organization gets started down such a path, they start to build an *investment position*—either a financial investment or a time investment or an emotional investment—in this issue. And soon they will want to defend that investment. So inadvertently they become new foot soldiers in this battle for bigger government.

The final concern is the relative comparison of uncertainty in trading values versus that in the basic global warming sciences. The authors appropriately salute uncertainty analysis in their paper. They suggest that in trading contracts, differences over plus or minus 5% are significant and differences over plus or minus 8-10% are not acceptable. However the mention of error bars of this magnitude is ironic in the sense that the error bars on the background science behind the global warming issue are so much larger than this plus or minus 8-10%.

Uncertainties in Global Warming Analysis

What follows are three brief reports on uncertainties in the global warming sciences.

(1) The work by Schwartz[5, 6] would suggest a range of at least -120% to +50%. This reference gives an excellent overview of the estimated contribution of various climate forcing variables including greenhouse gases, aerosols[7] and solar variability. The mean overall forcing for the past century or so of changes was about 2.7 watts/meter^2 with an uncertainty range from -0.6 up to 4 watts/meter^2. This 2.7 watts/meter^2 can be compared to the 238 watts/meter^2 of solar energy flux absorbed by the Earth.

(2) More recently another scientist, Dr. Sallie Baliunas, of the Harvard-Smithsonian Center for Astrophysics, testified[8] on factors in general circulation models (GCMs) that would suggest this uncertainty range was even much larger than that reported by Schwartz. For years modelers—particularly when they coupled atmospheric circulation models with ocean circulation models around 1993—required large flux adjustments at the ocean-atmosphere interface. In Chapter 3 we noted the coining of the phrase "fudge factors" for these adjustments. By 1998 some improvements in these GCMs had been made and the first GCM was announced that did not need such factors. Yet this new model still was making very unacceptably high errors. Further publications[9, 10] in 2002 and 2003 indicated that there was still continued use of these so-called flux adjustments.

The errors of concern here were the treatment of humidity, cloud cover and the equator to polar energy flow. This modeling can give rise to area by area flux adjustments as much as 25 times larger than the forcing from greenhouse gases.

(3) The third input on error analysis was reported in World Climate Report, a well known newsletter that covers the panorama of subjects that fall within the field of climate change. The editor of this newsletter, Patrick Michaels, professor of Environmental Sciences, University of Virginia and the Virginia State Climatologist, is a prominent and persistent critic of the GCMs. He has noted that "Since the models and the models alone are the linchpin of the whole greenhouse warming scare, very careful scrutiny of the models is required[11]."

His recent input on error analysis is for hindcasts for cloud cover over the period 1979 to 1988. It showed an incredibly broad error range applies to other predicted climate variables besides temperature. This study showed a plot of mean cloud cover (which ranged from 0 to 100%) by latitude bands, from 90N to 90S, comparing actual data vs computer results from 31 GCMs. Yes, there are now 31 different models. The model results spanned over almost all of the graph space. For example results from the 31 different models ranged from:

- for Houston (latitude, ~29N) a low of 15% coverage up to 70% versus a 55% actual value.

- for Anchorage (latitude, ~ 60N) a low of 20% coverage up to 95% versus a 60% observed.

Which model would one believe? Or why not just throw darts?

Conclusions

This very brief overview of the error situation on the global warming issue leads to the conclusion that such activities as emissions trading or emission credits are, at best, very premature. Let us press ahead on the scientific front and get the science right first. When that is accomplished we will be in a far better position to decide which is the best policy mix makes sense for the future.

References and Notes

(1) Part of this essay was first published as a letter to the Oil & Gas Journal, March 15, 1999.

(2) McCann T., and Magee, P., *Crude Oil Greenhouse Gas Life Cycle Analysis Helps Assign Values for CO_2 Emission Trading*, Oil and Gas Journal, February 22 1999.

(3) One cubic meter of a liquid fuel is equivalent to 6.3 barrels.

(4) See Chapter 3 for details on the Houston Forum debate on global warming. At the end of the debate, six out of the seven scientists involved indicated they would not sign the Kyoto Protocol. A key reason was an indication that even a full implementation of the treaties provisions by all countries, would reduce expected warming over the next century by only about 0.2° C.

(5) Schwartz, S. et al, *Uncertainties in Climate Change caused by Aerosols*, Science, May 24, 1996.

(6) *More data needed to support or disprove global warming*, Oil & Gas Journal, May 26, 1997, page 75. Provides another graph of the uncertainty data from (5) above.

(7) Aerosols are an important component of our atmosphere and play a key role in climate change. While the science of aerosols, like many of the fields in climate change, is incomplete, it is believed their presence has a predominantly opposite effect to the GHGs. Aerosols are very tiny particles, either liquid or solid, suspended in the air. If the particles are liquid the aerosol would be a mist or a fog. If the particles are solid the aerosol would be smoke or dust. A particular important aerosol is that formed from the presence of the sulfur dioxide molecule, SO_2. This molecule, whether from volcanoes or power plants, will ultimately become ionized and react with water vapor to create droplets of sulfurous and sulfuric acid. High in the atmosphere such very fine droplets of these compounds would contribute to the aerosol effect. Lower down in the atmosphere these would ultimately coalesce as acid rain.

Aerosols have received a tiny amount of attention compared to GHGs. Their potency can best be illustrated by the following example. An Indonesia eruption at Tambora, in 1815, was the largest eruption in the past 2,000 years. The aerosols produced from this event led, in 1816, to "the year without a summer" or "1816 and froze to death" in New England and eastern Canada.

Yet the science in this field is still embryonic. A recent write-up[12] made the statement: "No scientist has a clue to how much cooling actually is caused by the aerosols."

(8)   Baliunas, S., *Uncertainties in Climate Modeling: Solar Variability and Other Factors,* George C. Marshall Institute, September 17, 1996. See: www.marshall.org/article.php?id=12&print=1.

(9)   McKitrick, Ross, *Asking the Right Questions About Climate Change and the Kyoto Protocol,* Fraser Forum, February, 2002.
See: http://oldfraser.lexi.net/publications/forum/2002/02/section_10.html.

(10) Bast, Joseph L., *Eight Reasons Why 'Global Warming' is a Scam,* Heartland Institute, February 1, 2003. See: www.heartland.org/Article.cfm?artId=11548.

(11) World Climate Report, *The Very Model of a Modern Major GCM,* February 15, 1999.

(12) *Trying Times,* CO2 & Climate Newsletter, September 17, 2004.
See www.co2andclimate.org/wca/2004/wca_23c.html.

8. *The Invasion of the Gorons-IV: Emergence & Submergence of Tom Daschle*

Introduction

There are two objectives for this brief essay. The first is to alert your readers of the spotting of a key new Goron[1] This Goron goes by the name of Tom Daschle, and claims to be from South Dakota. But in reality he is from the planet Gore. The second objective of this report is to suggest a possible solution on how to silence this Goron, figuratively speaking of course. On second thought, there is no way to silence him, hence the objective should be to expose him to the public for what he has become: the abominable NO man. In other words to neutralize him. Now I'm sure this is not a new idea. Hence the value of this input will be in the approach to use, which will follow shortly.

As I write this report, the Head Goron has grown a beard, not the size of a Taliban beard mind you, but at least moving in that direction. There are however reports that he may have shaved it off. More on this beard later. In contrast our president, George W. Bush, and his Secretary of Defense, Donald Rumsfeld have had a few more weighty subjects on their platter, such as prosecuting a war against terror and terrorists.

The Battle in the Senate—New Gorons Emerge

In spite of losing the presidential election in 2000, the Gorons have had some highlights in 2001. When that election was over in November, the Republicans had control of the Senate by a 51 to 50 majority, with VP Dick Cheney casting any tie braking vote. Then two new Gorons emerged. Certainly Daschle was one of these, but momentarily more important, was the defection of Senator Jim Jeffords from Vermont, giving control of the Senate to the Democrats. Long known as a moderate, he had been labeled as "Clinton's favorite

Republican[4]", because of the number of times he had voted Democratic. Hence one should have suspected that he was a Goron. His defection still shocked some Republicans.

The defection will end up being the high point in Jeffords career. According to one well known Washington commentator he has switched "from being a Republican to being a Nothing[5]." His opinion will not be in demand. He will not be trusted by anyone. How can one trust a man who has been a member of Trent Lott's "Singing Senators [6]" barbershop quartet group, only to *stab* Lott in the back by his defection? He will not be a part of the Democratic inner circle. He may even be more forgotten as a Democrat than he was as a Republican.

Lott suggested that this defection would not change much in the Senate. But, first of all, in case he hasn't noticed, he lost his job as the Senate leader to Daschle. Is it possible that Lott may have been acknowledging here that he wasn't accomplishing much as the Senate leader? Secondly, the chairmen of the Senate committees are now Democrats, and these chairmen determine what gets debated and what gets voted on. For example Senator Frank Murkowski, from Alaska, will no longer be chairman of the Energy and Natural Resources Committee, and hence would have less influence on the future of the Arctic National Wildlife Refuge (ANWR). He will be replaced by a Jeff Bingaman, a New Mexico Democrat. This means that the President's energy bill in general, and the *free the ANWR* movement in particular, will now be under the management of the Democrats in the senate. Further, the defection of Jeffords pushes Daschle into the spotlight, becoming the new Democratic leader of the Senate. It strengthens his position in the Democratic party, tremendously, which was already pretty strong.

Senator Daschle: the new Leader of the Senate.

Daschle has taken up the challenge of being the Senate leader "with great zest, excoriating the presidents policies as profligate lunacy[5]." It soon became crystal clear, after he took over the leadership of the senate, that Tom Daschle was indeed a Goron. He probably has always been a Goron, but he has been able to disguise his heritage remarkably well.

After September 11 the Democrats agreed unanimously to support President Bush in the foreign policy arena. Any attacks had to be limited to domestic issues. Count on them to carp about every domestic issue for the next three years. President Bush "once imagined that the Sept. 11 terrorist attacks produced a bipartisan climate.... These illusions were dispelled the past three months[7]." Since that infamous date Democrats have battled "him remorselessly on domestic questions". Leading this diatribe against the

Whatever It Is I'm Against It!
by Bert Kalman and Harry Ruby

Stanza I
I don't know what they have to say.
It makes no difference anyways.
Whatever it is.
I'm against it.
No matter what it is or who commenced it.
I'm against it.

Stanza II
Your proposition may be good.
But lets have one thing understood.
Whatever it is.
I'm against it.
And even when you've changed it or condensed it.
I'm against it.

Chorus
I'm opposed to it.
On general principles, I'm opposed to it.
He's opposed to it
In fact, indeed,—
He's opposed to it.

Stanza III
For months before my son was born.
I used to yell from night to morn.
Whatever it is.
I'm against it.
And I've kept yelling since I first commenced it.
I'm against it.

President will be Dr. No[8] himself, Tom Daschle.

One example of this is Daschle's proposed energy bill that would prohibit drilling in ANWR, directly in opposition to the President's approach. While Daschle may talk about energy independence, Patrich Michaels, in his essay, *Energy Illogic,* indicated "his bill is a fake.... We didn't cause Sept. 11 by driving cars. Pure out-and-out hatred did, and hatred, too, knows no logic[9]."

Another example is the economic stimulus package. As the Christian Science Monitor noted: "Mr Daschle is currently playing chicken with President Bush over who will compro-mise[10]." Larry Kudlow also noted that Senator Daschle is "Reprising Al Gore's campaign mantra of bashing rich people and attacking business." Senator Daschle has opposed such ideas as accelerating income-tax cuts.

Kudlow observed this "would have truly provided anti-recession, economic-growth incentives". Daschle also opposed "the Bush plan for a 30% cash-bonus for immediate expencing of business depreciation write-offs". Again Kudlow noted these "would have significantly improved the outlook for the technology sector[11]."

An Approach to the Neutralization of Dr. No.

Rest assured, Senator Daschle will not go away, so the need continues to find a mechanism or strategy to cope with his tactics in general, and with his attacks and rejections in particular.

The use of music, poetry or lyrics has an impact worth a thousand words of precise, but dry prose. For example the Rush Limbaugh program frequently uses this technique with quality conversions of various songs to a more political set of lyrics. Further, in a prior report, the creative genius of many a timely and focused limerick[12] was noted. Recently another input came across my path, that is of the same quality as this limerick. But more than that, out of all possible songs, it could not be a better fit to attach to Mr. Daschle. Hence I believe it can be of great utility as we do battle with the Gorons. This input was from the lyrics to a movie theme, from one of the Marx Brothers movies, entitled *Horse Feathers*. The songs title is: *Whatever It Is, I'm Against It!*. The lyrics to this gem, at least as best as I can determine from an audio file[13] are listed.

In the movie theater, Groucho Marx, acting the role of a college professor, sang this song. In the political theater, I would propose we have Mr. Daschle, acting the role of a Senate leader, singing this song, or something like it. Perhaps we could create a new Groucho Marx.

Perhaps the GOP could develop one or two commercials built around the lyrics and the Groucho Marx image. For example, one commercial could be built around the first stanza and another around the second stanza. Individual Republicans could include some of these concepts in every speech they give. And Trent Lott could get his barbershop quartet fired up again, minus one notable Senator from Vermont, using this song—modified as necessary—anywhere and everywhere.

These lyrics—again modified as necessary—should be used over and over as the perfect, but simple, squelch to whatever point Dr No. has just pontificated on.

References and Notes

(1)   Parts of this essay were first published at eco-logic on-line, January 1, 2002.

(2-3) *Not assigned.*

(4)   Anderson, Kevin, *Q&A: What the Senate Switch Means*, BBC News, June 7, 2001.

(5)   Snow, Tony, *The Best Break*, TownHall.com. June 1, 2001.
       See: www.townhall.com/columnists/tonysnow/ts20010601.shtml

(6)   According to PBS, in May 2001,the members of this group were John Ashcroft, Larry Craig, Jim Jeffords and Trent Lott.

(7)   Novak, R., *GOP not cowering to Daschle's charm*, as published in the Houston Chronicle, December 25, 2001.

(8)   Brooks, D., *Tom Daschle, Dr. No*, The Weekly Standard, December 31 2001. See:
       www.weeklystandard.com/Content/Public/Articles/000/000/000/721zlmri.asp.

(9)   Michaels, P., *Energy Illogic*, Cato Institute, December 8, 2001.
       See: www.cato.org/dailys/12-08-01.html.

(10) *Daschle, Prairie Fireball*, Christian Science Monitor, December 21, 2001.
       See: www.csmonitor.com/2001/1221/p12s1-comv.htm

(11) Kudlow, L., *On Daschle's Deaf Ears*, National Review, December 21 2001.
       See: www.nationalreview.com/kudlow/kudlow.shtml.

(12) Duplantier, F., *Recount Dracula*, Eco-Logic On-Line, December 15, 2000.

(13) The lyrics for the theme song, from the movie, *Horse Feathers*, namely *"Whatever It Is I'm Against It"*, were extracted from: www.geocities.com/~jbenz/marxbros.html. No guarantee is made that these lyrics are complete. Also in one spot, where the chorus is singing "He's opposed to it", could not capture every word.

9. The Invasion of the Gorons-V: The Revenge of the Gorons

Introduction

It was bound to happen sooner or later. Surely the Clinton/Gore Administration left the bureaucracy full of angry Gorons[1]. Angry for the basic election results. Angry for Florida. Angry for the Supreme Court vote. And very angry for President Bush's position[2] on Kyoto. They wanted revenge. They needed revenge. And they would sit angrily waiting for the opportunity to sandbag the President.

It came in early June in 2002, probably due to the President being preoccupied with the War on Terror and Homeland Defense issues. It would seem he and his staff did not read the EPA report—entitled the Climate Action Report for 2002 (CAR2002)[3]—that, by treaty, is sent to the UN each year. This is incredible, knowing the tightrope Bush is trying to walk on this issue, and knowing the propensity for the Gorons to pile on the second there is an opening. "You'd think the Administration would know better than to hand the green lobby such an easy target. In February when Mr. Bush laid out a voluntary plan for reducing emissions, environmentalists wrote it off as 'window dressing'. They have now seized on the EPA report as an 'admissions' and are renewing calls for Kyoto[4]."

While the conclusions of the EPA report were consistent with his global warming program, the guts of the report had some damaging statements, now included in an official U.S. report. These statements will likely come back to haunt the Administration through the balance of this year, and indeed through the balance of his term, unless somehow, this report could be withdrawn.

The Liberal Media Has a Field Day.

Many news reports suggested that the Bush Administration had done another flip flop on global warming. For example the New York Times headline declared: "Climate Changing U. S. Says in Report." And in the sub-headline: "Bush Administration, in Shift, Predicts Global Warming[5]." This EPA report, released as the official position of the U. S., now concedes we will see more drought, more damage to coastal areas, more public health problems and severe damage to a variety of ecosystems. And all of these problems, according to this report, are primarily due to human actions, such as combustion of fossil fuels in factories, homes and vehicles. These so-called conclusions are in sharp contrast to previous responses by this Administration on climate change, which always included the conclusion that the science was incomplete and much more research was needed. Now it is going to be extremely difficult for skeptics to raise the argument against the Gorons that the science is too early stage to be the basis for any policy changes. The Administration, at least according to this official U. S. report has adopted the tenuous position that "global warming is a disaster in the making and then refuses to help solve the problem, especially when solutions are so clear[5]." Well not hardly, but that is the claim of this report. Previously the Administration had described climate change as a serious issue. Now it emerges as a serious problem.

In another report, the headlines in the Houston Chronicle, declared there is a "changing stance at White House on climate change." In the body of this report the AP claimed the Administration "puts most of the blame for recent warming on human activities. Human induced warming and associated sea level rise are expected to continue through the 21st century. Secondary effects include increases in rainfall rates and increased susceptibility of semiarid regions to drought. There is general agreement that the observed warming is real and has been particularly strong within the past 20 years[6]."

Environmentalists see this report as the basis for a change in the Administration's climate change plan. "It's good they have done a 180 degree turn on the science. "But we're still waiting for a plan that mandates pollution cuts." In this situation pollution means carbon dioxide.

The Dismay of the Skeptics.

It didn't take the skeptics more than a couple of nano seconds to realize the White House had made a gigantic blunder. Indeed the President, within a day of the release of CAR2002, started to distance himself from this report, calling it a *product of the bureaucracy*. The White House staff at times displays some rather Neanderthal characteristics. Unfortunately, this was such an occasion.

Hear the concerns of these skeptics.

- Dr. Sallie Baliunas[7] is an astrophysicist and an astronomer. She observed that while news reports, particularly the report in the New York times on this new EPA release, suggests there has been a breakthrough on global warming science. This breakthrough, at least according to the Gorons, completes the research—the science is now finished and the impact is clear: global warming is happening, it is caused by humans and it will damage our nation. Baliunas assures us there has been no new science at all. She goes on to further state that the sciences prove exactly the opposite of the claims in this EPA report and indeed demonstrates that greenhouse gases are not the cause of global warming.

She notes that this EPA report relies heavily on selected scenarios being presented on what might happen to our nation. Last year a National Academy of Sciences (NAS) Panel, in it's Report to the President, pointed out "that the future scenarios about weather and changing systems were among the most uncertain areas of unsettled science of climate change." Dr Richard Lindzen (see Chapter 3), a member of this NAS panel, called these forecasts a "children's exercise" based on "thinking of all the bad things that could be said that global warming might cause." Baliunas concluded with the observation that *Science* demands that ideas be tested. And the testing of the human based global warming hypothesis has, so far, failed such tests.

- Fred Singer is an environmental scientist. Immediately after seeing the New York Times report on the CAR2002, he wrote to the Times. While the paper published his letter, it was edited extensively from about 425 words down to slightly more than 100 words. He commented that while this EPA report "may well claim a current climate warming from human activities, but that does not make it true." Singer went on: "the balance of the observational evidence certainly does not support such a claim[8]." It would appear the EPA authors, unquestionably full fledged Gorons, have simply rehashed a highly discredited report put out by the Clinton-Gore Administration—the National Assessment of Future Impacts of Climate Change or NACC. Such studies are based on GCM results. As Chapter 7 noted that there are 31 GCMs and the NACC is based on probably the two weakest climate models around. The outputs from these models frequently disagree with each other, with both likely being wrong. Singer noted that the EPA report to the UN is a routine document, updated yearly. It does not list the specific Gorons responsible, nor their qualifications.

Next Singer submitted a letter to the President, signed by more than 30 individuals and organizations, expressing concerns on the EPA report. This letter characterized the CAR2002 as a "compilation and summary of junk science produced by the Clinton/Gore Administration in order to support their Kyoto agenda." The CAR2002 report is based extensively on the NACC report, which was so offensive and biased that your Administration stated on September 6, 2001 that it was "not policy positions or official statements of the U. S. government." This was part of the settlement of legal action brought by three members of congress and several of the organizations signing this letter. This letter to the President concluded that the CAR2002 "undermines your position on the Kyoto Protocol and damages effort in the Congress to advance your energy policies and to oppose environmental policies that would implement Kyoto-style constraints on energy use." It further called on the President to withdraw the CAR2002 and to order it to be rewritten based on sound science.

- Steve Milloy is a writer and adjunct scholar at the Cato Institute. Milloy also noted that the scientific basis for CAR2002 was the NACC report, which was issued barely 10 days before the 2000 election to try and help Albert Gore Jr. win. As a result of this duplicity the Competitive Enterprise Institute (CEI), along with Senator James Inhofe (R, OK), Representative Joe Knollenberg (R, MI), Representative Jo Ann Emerson (R, MO) and several others filed a lawsuit against the Clinton Administration charging that this NACC report was unlawfully prepared. This suit was settled in September 2001 by the Bush Administration, "which agreed to withdraw the NACC report and acknowledge the report isn't official U. S. government policy[9]." However once a report, that the Gorons like, is in print, even though it is highly discredited, it will never go away.

- James K. Glassman is also a writer and publisher. It would appear he is of the opinion the CAR2002 will also never go away. He concludes the "stage is set for an inevitable government-run program to cut carbon-dioxide emissions by cutting energy use[10]." In allowing this report to be issued the President is essentially accepting the basic premises of the extreme environmentalists. As a result "the President will ultimately be forced to accept the major content of the same treaty that he rejected a little over a year ago as 'fatally flawed.'" Clearly Glassman is rather pessimistic about this development.

The NACC Report.

Since the CAR2002 is based so extensively on the NACC report a more detailed review of that report is in order. The NACC study relied on two computer models. The first was from the Hadley Center for Climate Prediction and Research in Britain. The second model was from the Canadian Center for Climate Modeling and Research. Some of the problems with these models include:

(1) Model Discrepancies. The discrepancy between the two models is astounding. For example in one model the Dakotas lose 85% of their average rainfall, while the second model shows they pick up 75%.

(2) Model Discrepancies. Another example: temperature forecasts for Alaska are between 5 to 12 °F degrees of warming via the British model and 7 to 18 °F degrees for the Canadian.

(3) Forecast Logic. The logic is not sound in some cases. For example one prediction for the southeast claimed that this "region's heat index is likely to rise more dramatically than anywhere else in the USA." One Report argues these forecasts "strain the realms of physical possibility[11]." In particular, the Canadian model projects July heat index values of better than 120 °F across much of the region. Yet it is very very rare for this index to exceed 120 °F for even a single day. Even in the most uncomfortable locations in this region this index, on average exceeds 105 °F on about 12 days per year. It is near impossible to produce a temperature/humidity combination that yields an index value over 120 °F. The reason is that so much heat is used up in the evaporation of the high moisture load, rather "than heating up the thermometer".

Hear what some skeptics have had to say about the NACC report:

- Patrick J. Michaels, a state climatologist, prolific writer and speaker, argues that the NACC report "has turned out to be one of the most misleading publicly funded reports on climate change this nation has ever produced." The writer notes that the two models used can't reproduce observed climate. "In addition to large scale inaccuracies, the models' spatial resolution is too coarse to include most small-scale processes…the type of processes that are responsible for local weather patterns[12]."

- Fred Singer, in his testimony[13] before the Senate Committee on Commerce, Science and Transportation, made several points:

  (1) There is no significant warming as indicated by
    a) satellite data,
    b) balloon data and
    c) surface based data for the continental USA.

  (2) The absence of a warming trend, as noted in the above three data bases, should serve to discredit any predictions from the current set of climate models.

  (3) The two models used in the NACC report are known to produce more extreme forecasts than the balance of the models.

Singer concludes that regional climate forecasts are outside the state of the art, and as one would expect, are more unbelievable than even the global average forecasts. As such the NACC report has produced numbers disguised as forecasts. But the models/process are so badly flawed that these numbers provide no basis for public policy or regional planning.

- A report by the *Cooler Heads Coalition* noted that the criticism was not limited to that from skeptics. Some scientists in both the IPCC and the EPA came out against this effort. For example two EPA scientists, who oversaw the Health Sector Work Group, stated that the overview of the health chapter is "*scientifically suspect*[14]." Their concerns follow:

(1) "Statements about health and climate change are alarmist and unsupported by the actual health sector analysis and text."

(2) "Overstates the potential impact of climate change on public health and understates the already existing need for public health infrastructures."

(3) "Contains scientifically inaccurate statements about the potential implication of climate change for air pollution and human health. Text that was carefully crafted by the human health sector lead authors was altered by the National Assessment Synthesis Team, leading to significant inaccuracies."

(4) Contains statements about vector-borne diseases that the lead authors (particularly experts from CDC) do not concur with."

The two EPA scientists indicated if these problems were not corrected they would "recommend that EPA not concur on the release of this document. The scientific credibility of the assessment process is at stake."

Conclusions

Well the Gorons have had their fun. They now have an official report that states about every thing they would like declared on global warming. There is no sign of any action that would lead to the withdrawal of this report. Expect the Gorons to use this report at every possible opportunity including the upcoming Rio + 10 meeting, and the November elections. It also strengthens the efforts of states such as California to move ahead of the federal government on this issue.

An example of what to expect was delivered by John Kerry, Senator from Massachuset, who charged the Administration "of engaging in a 'useless, ceaseless stupid fight' against the Kyoto climate change pact[15]."

Surely the fight must go on. It will be much more difficult, but not impossible. Fortunately the EPA report comes with a multiplicity of caveats about the uncertainties in the science of climate change. This report did recognize that "any definitive prediction of potential outcomes is not yet feasible." Also it noted that "one of the weakest links in our knowledge is the connection between global and regional predictions of climate change[16]." Finally President Bush has repeatedly stated he opposes the Kyoto Protocol, the latest occasion when he called this EPA report a *product of the bureaucracy*.

The ultimate victor in this battle will be that political party that can handle or finesse this issue the most effectively. The Gorons already have a lead based on their ability as master rhetoriticians, plus the incredible support they receive from the media. And this event gives them more ammunition than they ever have had. Hence, the Invasion of the Gorons is about to enter a new phase. The global warming skeptics, along with those of conservative persuasion, must rise to this situation like never before. This is a call to arms. "Now is the time for all good men to come to the aid of their country." "Man the Barricades." "Once more to the breach." "Remember the Alamo." And so on. This fight was never going to be easy, and now it has been made much harder, but it is not an impossible fight.

References and Notes

(1)   Part of this essay was published initially at eco-logic on-line, August 1, 2002.

(2)   See www.epa.gov/globalwarming/news/speeches/gwbush_021402.html for President Bush's position[2] on the Kyoto Protocol.

(3)   The EPA Climate Action Report for 2002 is available at: www.epa.gov/globalwarming/publications/car/index.html.

(4)   Wall Street Journal, Review & Outlook: *More Hot Air on Kyoto*, June 5, 2002.

(5)   Revkin, Andrew C., *Climate Changing, U. S. Says in Report. Bush Administration, in Shift, Predicts Global Warming*, New York Times, June 3, 2002.

(6)   Associated Press, *Changing Stance at White House on Climate Change*, Houston Chronicle, June 4, 2002.

(7)   Baliunas is an astrophysicist at the Harvard-Smithsonian Center for Astrophysics, and Deputy Director of the Mount Wilson Observatory. She is also co-host of Tech Central Station. See: *Get Out the Ouija Boards*, www.techcentralstation.com, June 4, 2002.

(8)   Singer is Professor Emeritus, University of Virginia and President of the Science & Environmental Policy Project. He is the founder and editor of the on-line newsletter: That Was the Week That Was (TWTW). See TWTW for June 8, 2002.

(9)   Milloy is the publisher of www.junkscience.com, which was noted by Popular Science as one of 50 best web sites. This site is dedicated to illuminating the inadequacies and politics in scientific research. Milloy has four degree in bioscience and law. He is author or co-author of several books on this subject. See: *Global Warming Fears Must Cool Down*, Fox News Channel, June 7, 2002.

(10) James Glassman is also co-host for Tech Central Station. See: *Say It Ain't So, George*, www.techcentralstation.com, June 3, 2002.

(11) *Assessing the Assesment—Southeast Fantasy*, World Climate Report, Vol 6, No. 22, July 23, 2001. See: www.greeningearthsociety.org/climate/V6n22/assess1.htm.

(12) Michaels is professor of Environmental Sciences at the University of Virginia, past president of the American Association of State climatologists, a senior fellow at the Cato Institute, author or co-author of several books and editor of *World Climate Report*, a publication of the Greening Earth Society See: Assessing the Assesment—Model Behavior?, World Climate Report, Vol 6, No. 20, June 25, 2001, at www.greeningearthsociety.org/climate/V6n22/assess1.htm.

(13) Singer, F., *National Assessment of the Potential Impact of Climate Change: Climate Change Impacts on the United States*, Testimony before the Senate Committee on Commerce, Science and Transportation, July 8, 2000. See: www.sepp.org/NewSEPP/senatetestimony.htm.

(14) The Cooling Heads Coalition is a sub-group of the National Consumer Coalition. It was formed in 1997 to help better define the global warming situation by exposing flawed scientific, economic and risk analysis. See: *EPA Blasts the National Assessment*, Cooler Heads, Vol.IV, No. 10, May 17, 2000.

(15) Dunne, Nancy, *The Americas: Bush warned on global warming*, Financial Times, July 12, 2002. See: www.ft.com.

(16) Seelye, Katharine Q., *President Distances Himself from Global Warming Report*, New York Times, June 5, 2002.

10. The *Hockey Stick*, the Little Ice Age and the Medieval Warming Period

Introduction—Recent Climate Change

There have been many reports and letters to the editors, by proponents[1] of the global warming issue, that claim we are experiencing unprecedented climate change. Today, every major weather event will receive unlimited media coverage. These reports will frequently couple the event to global warming. Perhaps the most egregious reports[2a,2b] about this *unprecedented climate change* is that for the *hockey stick* profile. This profile shows 950 years of temperature history as flat to slightly declining (the stick), followed by a dramatic rise over the past 50 years (the blade). More on this shortly.

> **Box 1—Life in the 14th Century[7]**
>
> *A physical chill settled on the 14th century at its very start, initiating the miseries to come. The Baltic Sea froze over twice, in 1303 and 1306-07; years followed of unseasonable cold, storms and rains, and a rise in the level of the Caspian Sea. Contemporaries could not know it was the onset of what has since been recognized as the **Little Ice Age**. Nor were they yet aware that, owing to the climatic change, communications with Greenland were gradually being lost, that the Norse settlements there were being extinguished, that cultivation of grain was disappearing from Iceland and being severely reduced in Scandinavia. But they could feel the colder weather, and mark with fear its result: a shorter growing season. This meant disaster, for population in the last century had already reached a delicate balance with agriculture techniques. In 1315, after rains so incessant that they were compared to the Biblical flood, crops failed all over Europe, and famine, the dark horseman of the Apocalypse, became familiar to all.*
>
> *"No epoch was more mutually mad". The 14th was a time of ferocity and spiritual agony, a world plunged into chaos. These are the years when the Black Death struck in the great plague of 1348-1350, killing more than a third of the entire population between India and Iceland, and returned four times during the rest of the century...when freebooting companies of brigands terrorized Europe with impunity...when a "hundred years' war" seemed to have no beginning and no end, and, defying the belligerents' own efforts to end it, acquired a life of its own.*
>
> *In the next 50 years...the Black Death disappeared, but...depopulation reached its lowest point in a society already weakened both physically and morally.*

The charge is repeatedly made, or implied, that this climate change is due solely to society's activities. One writer, a Bill McKibben, argues these changes are not small. He has been most prolific[3] in this effort. His concerns include such items as:

- *Spring coming a week earlier in the Northern Hemisphere.* Nowhere does he offer any evidence that this event is caused by society. No mention was made that this could just as well be a product of natural climate variation. Nor does he go in to any possible benefits from this development[4].

- *10% more vegetation above the 45th parallel since 1980.* For those who understand photo-synthesis this development would not come as a surprise[5]. Again he does not go in to any possible benefits from this development.

- *Now the world's climatologists say, with near unanimity, that the planet is heating up and that we are the cause.* This statement by McKibben is probably the most outrageous of all he has made. This claim ignores[6a] the position of many key individual climatologists, meteorologists or other scientists that are concerned skeptics. It ignores the various declarations[6b] by climatologists, including the American Association of State Climatologists. And finally it ignores the largest petition[6c] conducted of knowledgeable scientists, engineers and others on this subject.

Objective

The objective here will be a critique of the hockey stick profile and a defense of the prior historians view of a warm period followed by a cold period and now followed by another warm period. Our climate history is rich with stories of incredible climate change. This 1000 year period is long enough to show that such devastating climate change has occurred, completely independent of society's activities. This period is also recent enough to be relatively well covered by history and to have some familiarity with most readers.

Historian's Views on Recent Past Climates—Background

Rather than listen to how prolific writers from the environmental movement discuss climate change, it is preferable to see what professional historians have had to say about this subject. The first historian is Barbara Tuchman[7], followed by some inputs from Hubert Lamb[8a]. As a third source, historical inputs from the UN are also included.

Box 1 is a summary of Tuchman's writings on the 14th century. This material was written over 20 years ago. She notes that the 14th century was the start of the Little Ice Age (LIA). This LIA saw a rather dramatic cooling from a warmer era, known as the Medieval Warming Period (MWP). The MWP covered several hundred years up to the 14th century.

Perhaps no other writer has covered climate history—and in particular the MWP and the LIA—more extensively than H. H. (Hubert) Lamb. His research[8a] is used extensively in this report. Among his many achievements was the founding and the initial directing of the Climatic Research Unit, University of East Anglia. Lamb passed away in 1997 as perhaps the greatest climatologist[8b] of his time. He might be viewed as the father of the study of climate change.

Finally, the 1990 and the 1995 Intergovernmental Panel on Climate Change (IPCC) *determined that the mean air temperature of the globe most likely varied as shown* in Figure 1[9]. This temperature graph is deduced from weather records and a variety of proxy climate data. While this graph has the look of precision, there surely are major uncertainties incorporated in it. However it is supported by, and consistent with a very large number of anecdotal inputs. Yet today, the IPCC is walking away from this view without any explanation or debate. In contrast Daly[10] argues *if the IPCC today were more objective they would involve historians everywhere to research their resources to determine past climates as observed and experienced by human societies.*

The Medieval Warming Period

The warmer conditions associated with the MWP are known to have had a

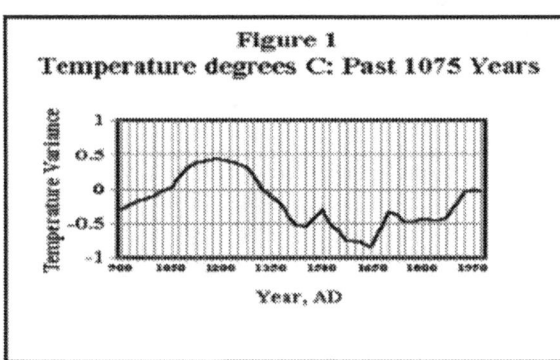

largely beneficial impact on both animals and plants. These conditions were so favorable that this period is often referred to as the *Little Climate Optimum*. After 800 AD there was no doubt[8a] that the climate in Europe was warming. In Europe temperatures are believed to have reached some of the warmest levels[8a] of the last 4000 years. The conditions during the MWP were such that:

- More and more trips into the North Atlantic occurred. Records show that Irish monks settled on the Faeroe Islands around 700 AD, and visited Iceland in 790 AD.

- A substantial part of the Arctic ice pack retreated north, allowing the settlement of Iceland and Greenland. The first recorded Viking trip to Iceland came in 860 AD. Cultivation of grain started immediately and continued into the 14th century. The first Viking settlement in Greenland was started about 980 AD. This warm phase reached it's peak in Greenland in the 12th century.

- Exploration of the Labrador coastline occurred somewhere between 980 and 1000AD. A modest settlement at L'Anse aux Meadows was established about1000AD.

- Alpine passes, normally blocked year around with snow and ice, became functional. This allowed trade between Italy and Germany to flourish.

- Sufficient grape production was achieved to permit the emergence of a wine industry in England. Over the period from 1100 to 1300 AD, there seems to have been less threat from frost in the critical month of May.

Although the warm phase extended into the 1300's, the end of the MWP was at hand.

The Little Ice Age

The colder conditions, associated with the LIA, are known to have had a largely detrimental impact on both animals and plants. The 14th century was not the coldest of the years covered by the LIA, but this gave little comfort to those who were carving out an existence on the very margin of sustainable development. The change that occurred was enough to start to drive the inhabitants south, whether they were Eskimos or Iroquois or Vikings. And if they could not move south many of them would perish, primarily by starvation.

The coldest part of the LIA in Europe is believed to be around 1695 AD. One of the more incredible reports about this period indicate that, from 1690 to 1728, Eskimos in Kayaks, periodically showed up at the Orkney Islands and even northern Scotland.

Temperatures in Figure 1 show nearly a 1½° C (2¾° F) drop versus the high during the MWP. Again regional variations would exist. For example, for the interval from 1675 to 1705 AD, an area between Iceland and the Faeroe Islands was[9] about 5° C (9° F) colder than the modern average.

The conditions during the LIA were such that:

- Sea ice returned to the coast of Iceland in 1203 AD. Between 1200 and 1240 AD the growing of oats on Iceland was abandoned and the production of barley grain was cut in half.

- Sea ice surrounded parts of Ireland. Many reports also indicate the Dutch canals and the Thames River in England froze over. Both of these are now generally ice free year around.

- Severe storms and flooding occurred in Europe repeatedly with unbelievable casualties. The numbers reported would make the Galveston Hurricane look like a minor storm. The very cold North Atlantic created a strong thermal gradient between 50° and 65° N latitudes. This led to occasional cyclonic wind storms exceeding the severity of the worst storms of modern times. Lamb[8a] reports at least four sea floods of the Dutch and German coasts in the 13th century where the death toll exceeded 100,000. These tragedies were repeated in storms of 1421, 1446 and 1570. In the storm of 1570, great cities were flooded and the deaths were estimated at 400,000.

- The period from 1690 through 1700 has been called the coldest decade in Europe's recorded history. The tragic story[11] of Queen Anne may be of interest in this context. Queen Anne was pregnant 18 times from 1683 to 1700, but only five children were born alive and only one of these survived to the age of eleven. Could this have been due to her own poor health? Could this have been a reflection of the state of medical services at that time? Or could this be testimony to the fact that it was impossible to keep the stone castles of that era warm and dry?

- On March 6, 1716, the Aurora Borealis, also known as the Northern Lights, returned to England. Few, if any, had ever seen this phenomenon as it had been absent from these skies for over 70 years, since 1645 AD. "Frightened servants thronged the street convinced that the day of judgement had arrived[12]." Scientists now know this was the end of the Maunder Minimum, a period where sunspots on the surface of the sun virtually disappeared. Without these sunspots and the magnetic activity and the solar wind that came with them, the Northern Lights disappeared.

What was the cause of the MWP/LIA?

Three ideas are reviewed below. While listed separately it is possible these three all are interconnected. The hypothesis are:

- **Changes in atmospheric circulation.** Part of the explanation[8a] of the MWP, in Europe and North America, must be that there was a persistent tilt of the circumpolar vortex[13] away from the Atlantic towards the Pacific. The Pacific was then impacted by frequent intrusions of polar air.

- **Changes in oceanic circulation,** in part, the Gulf stream, more specifically in the so-called thermo-haline circulation[14] (THC). In a recent paper[15],

Wallace Broecker, the guru who popularized the THC, noted that *one of our tasks is to gain a better understanding of the Little Ice Age and its demise* and to confirm or refute that it was due to changes in the THC.

Do we understand why the THC has changed. Surely not in adequate detail. *Although short term variability in Atlantic climate is thought to be relatively well understood*[16] *both the patterns and the mechanisms of variability on decadal to century scales are as yet poorly known.*

•   **Changes in solar output.** It is well known that an 11 year sunspot cycle exists, but this period would seem to be too short for changes seen between the MWP and the LIA. It is also well known that many other solar cycles exist. For example, the 80—90 year Gleissberg cycle seems fairly clear in the sunspot record. Longer cycles, on the order of 150 to 300 years, are indicated in the geochemical record, and hinted at in the sunspot record with the Spoerer Minimum around 1500 AD, the Maunder Minimum at 1645 to 1715 and the Dalton Minimum at 1795 to 1825. These minima likely contributed to the LIA. They represent periods where the sunspot activity is at a very low level. Baliunas[17] believes these long-term lulls in activity could be the source of these longer term climate cycles. Finally the prospect of a 1500 year cycle has been raised[15].

The Hockey Stick Analysis

As one might expect the serious skeptics have been rather disturbed by Mann's reports in general, and the unquestioned acceptance of them by the mass media in particular. As this essay was in it's final stages, this writer attended a debate in Houston, where the proponent included a large version of Figure 2, on a scaffold, as part of his evidence. There was no discussion of it's basis and it's weaknesses. There was zero discussion of the very major uncertainties involved. It was presented as fact. How many other times and places has this graph been so used?

In a recent report[18], the author quotes Wallace Broecker, and noted that, since long term temperature fluctuations are about 1°C, that proxies must be accurate to 0.5°C to be useful over a 1000 year period. He also noted this rules out tree ring proxies as an acceptable input.

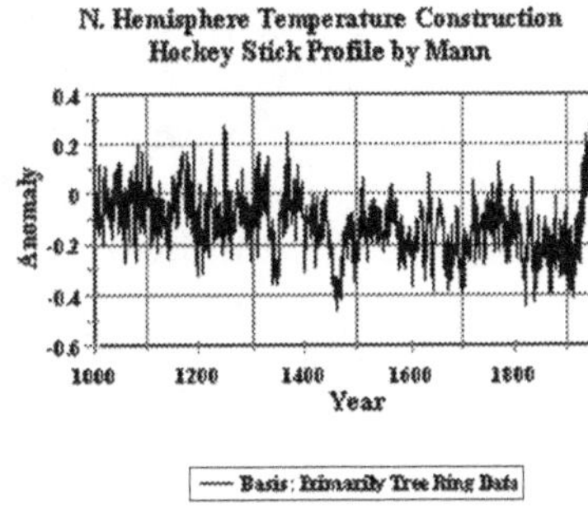

Three blocks follow that either critique the hockey stick analysis directly or comment on the state of global warming science.

Figure 2

N. Hemisphere Temperature Construction Hockey Stick Profile by Mann

Basis: Primarily Tree Ring Data

Block 1—Daly's Critique of the *Hockey Stick*. The first critique[10] is by John Daly—An Australian, His arguments are listed below.

While the developers of this hypothesis used a variety of temperature proxies, it is based almost entirely on tree ring data. Tree ring proxies are not sound indicators of the annual average temperature. They are proxies only for land based growth (~29 % of the planet), over daytime hours, during the growing season. Tree ring growth also depends on many other variables besides temperature: rainfall, sunlight, clouds, pests and nutrients. Conclusion: tree ring data provides a very weak base for temperature reconstructions.

Greenhouse advocates argue that proxies are better inputs than historical anecdotes. However Daly argues the wider academic community will grant much more credibility to well researched historical evidence. He argues it is inconceivable that the MWP/LIA could be observed so globally and yet be missed by Mann's study. He concludes that climate history bears no resemblance whatever to Mann's *hockey stick*.

Daly asks why there was so little challenge to Mann's hypothesis? And why is there collective denial to the alternative hypothesis e.g. the role of the sun?

Daly cites the National Academy of Sciences booklet on the code of scientists. It holds up the role of skeptics and the importance of skepticism. It treats it as a virtue, but in the global warming field, skeptics are treated with great hostility.

While Daly, and indeed this writer, are not opposed to the changing of conventional wisdom on any subject, it should be done with extensive, patient and wide open debate. This has not been the case here. Rather we are seeing change by omission, where the existing view is essentially ignored and this new view saluted over and over again by the environmental media and other proponents. They argue the MWP/LIA is defined as only a local phenomenon and hence not relevant. Daly refutes this claim with extensive global examples. Ironically the hockey stick research is based on Northern Hemisphere data.

Block 2—Inputs from The Center for the Study of Carbon Dioxide and Climate change. The critique by the Center for the Study of Carbon Dioxide and Climate Change is based on the fact that CO_2 is the raw material for biomass growth. They have pioneered in the area of positive impacts due to increased CO_2. Dr. Craig Idso and Dr. Keith Idso and their father, Dr. Sherwood Idso, have prepared a large number of editorials or summaries on topics of import to this field. For example:

- Editorial 4-1-99: *CO_2 and Temperature: The Great Geophysical Waltz*—So who leads who? It is definitely not CO_2. Sometimes they are totally out of harmony. When they are in harmony, it is temperature that seems to take the lead.

- Editorial 8-2-00: *Temperature Reconstructions Based on Plant—Climate Interactions are In-accurate if Atmospheric CO_2 varied Over the Period of Reconstruction.* QED.

- Editorial 2-7-01: *The Crux of the Climate Policy Debate*—Claim this is a price/tax on carbon.

- Editorial 2-14-01: *Elitist Leaders Out of Step with Scientific Reality*—The Idso's criticize David Gergen's editorial (U.S. News & World Report 2-5-01). Basis of Gergen's writing was a meeting of 3000 leaders in Davos Switzerland.

- Editorial 2-21-01: *The Most Important Global Change*—This is population growth along with the food, water and energy needs this will bring. The Idso's argue rather than reducing CO_2, we need to let it rise to boost food production.

Block 3 Inputs from SEPP—the Science & Environmental Policy Project. The third critique is based on the work of Fred Singer and his Science & Environmental Policy Project. Singer is an atmospheric physicist, professor emeritus of environmental sciences at the University of Virginia and the first director of the U. S. Weather Satellite Service. Like the Idso's, Singer has a web site—The Week that Was (TWTW)—and prepares and presents many essays each month. Singer concludes each weekly newsletter with the following quote by Thomas H. Huxley: "The improver of natural knowledge absolutely refuses to acknowledge authority as such. For him skepticism is the highest of duties: blind faith the one unpardonable sin." Examples of his concerns:

- Science 5-20-98: *Anthropogenic climate warming in the 20th century?* Reports on three temperature reconstructions, that show very different climate profiles since 1400 AD. The most significant differences are in the last 150 years.

- EOS 4-20-99: *Human Contribution to Climate Change Remains Questionable*—Reviews evidence. Notes "the observational evidence suggests that any warming from the growth of greenhouse gases is likely to be minor, difficult to detect above the natural fluctuations of the climate, and therefore in-consequential".

- The Christian Science Monitor, 8-24-00. (See also *TWTW@sepp.org*, 11-23-00): *Some Lessons from a Major Climate Change in Our Own Era*—Reports on the MWP/LIA with events from North America (Greenland, Ellsemere Island, Vinland, Alaska, and the Rocky Mountains), Europe (England, Iceland, Scotland, and mountain glaciers) and China.

Conclusions

Several conclusions can be drawn from this excursion into 1300 years of recent history:

(1) Simplistic explanations in this field of climate phenomenon should be avoided as the science is incredibly complex, evolving, and full of areas of either very high uncertainty or of outright propaganda. To truly understand this field, one needs many inputs from a variety of sources.

(2) It is not axiomatic that the higher up the governmental chain one travels, the better the inputs one gets. In particular, the readers are reminded that the IPCC is a UN organization, and inputs from it may come wrapped up in the UN agenda. While there is very good science inside many UN reports, what frequently gets the headlines are politically driven executive summaries and fancy news releases.

(3) Tree ring data, while useful for many applications, are not sound proxies for temperature reconstructions, such as the *hockey stick* profile. At the very best tree ring data represent less than 5 % of the temperature cover-age needed for a global average (29 % of the worlds area as land times about half the hours in a day and times about a third of the months in a year). Hence the existence of the MWP/LIA has not been disproven by this analysis, and the rush to shove the MWP/LIA aside should be halted.

(4) Far more research is needed to better understand the astrophysics, the bio-geo-chemical aspects, the meteorology, and the oceanography that interacts with our climate.

(5) Very real, natural climate variation phenomena are involved that have nothing to do with the emission of greenhouse gases in the 20th century.

(6) While the existence of strong natural climate variation forces surely does not disprove the conventional greenhouse warming theory, it is certainly food for thought.

(7) While it would be presumptuous to claim that all the problems encoun-tered over the past 1300 years were due to a cooling period, and all the positive developments were due to a warming period, there seems to be some teachings here. The teachings of history just might be that if one had to choose between global cooling and global warming, the warming side would be the side to choose.

References and Notes

(1) Parts of this essay appeared in 2002, as a guest editorial on the web site: Center for the Study of Carbon Dioxide and Global Change.

In this essay proponents, sometimes called warmers or global warmers, refer to those who believe that serious consequences are imminent unless mankind reduces its emissions of greenhouse gases immediately. Skeptics believe that the case for this scenario has yet to be made.

(2a) Mann, M., et al, *Global-scale temperature patterns and climate forcing over the past six centuries*, Nature, 392: 779-787, 1998. Mann's paper provides a temperature assessment, over the past millennium, that is primarily based on tree ring data. This reconstruction, sometimes referred to as *the hockey stick profile*, showed the decade of the 1990's as *the warmest of the Northern Hemisphere this millennium*. However the authors of this work indicate their reluctance to compare this analysis with the MWP, by limiting it, at least in this paper, to after 1400 AD.

(2b) Mann, M., et al, *Northern Hemisphere Temperatures During the Past Millennium: Inferences, Uncertainties and Limitations*, Geophysical Research Letters, **26**, 6, March 15, 1999.

(3) As an example of the writings of the omni present Bill McKibben, the following letters are cited. Not only does he write letters to the Editor, but appears to do it all across the country. Or perhaps he gets it done for him by a hired public relations firm. For example in spring of 1997, this writer noticed very similar letters by McKibben in the:

- New York Times, *The Earth Does a Slow Burn*, March 7, 1997
- Houston Chronicle, *Not the same planet Earth on which we were born*, June 19, 1997, and
- Dallas Morning News, *U. S. abandons promise to cut greenhouse gas emissions*, June 26, 1997.
- Further, one editorial—The Salt Lake Tribune, *Global Warming May Be Causing Wild Weather*, May 18, 1997—appeared to extract some of it's inputs from McKibbens writings.

It is a safe assumption that similar letters/editorials appeared in other newspapers across the USA.

(4) As one who grew up on the northern plains, what farmers have most worried about was not spring coming early, but coming late, or alternatively fall frost coming early. Tuchman, in Box 1, notes the same concern, namely a shorter growing season.

(5)   One area that proponents and skeptics agree on is the increased level of carbon dioxide (CO_2) in the atmosphere. Since CO_2 is the raw material of photosynthesis, it should not be a surprise that increased agricultural yields and forest growth have been widely reported. Why that is a negative is hard to comprehend.

(6a) Gray, W., Viewpoint: *Get Off the Global Warming Bandwagon*, BBC News, November 16, 2000. Dr. Gray is professor of Atmospheric Sciences at Colorado State University and the director of the foremost hurricane forecasting team in the world.

(6b) Cleary, P. (media contact), *Survey of State Climate Experts Casts Doubt on Link Between Human Activity and Global Warming*, Citizens for a Sound Economy, October 7, 1997.

(6c) Singer, F., *Kyoto Accord Protest Quickening*, Washington Times, April 22, 1998. This reference notes that 15,000 scientists, engineers and others, with at least 10,000 with advanced degrees signed this petition that urged the U. S. Government to reject the Kyoto Agreement. This petition, known as The Oregon Petition is now believed to be over 20,000.

(7)   Tuchman, B., *A Distant Mirror—The Calamitous 14th Century*, Alfred A. Knepf, 1978. Part of this description is from Chapter 2, and part is taken from the inside book cover.

(8a) Lamb, H., *Climate, Change and the Modern World*, 2nd ed., Routledge, London, New York, 1995.

(8b) Lamb, H., *Through all the Changing Scenes of Life—A Meteorologist's Tale*, Taverner Publishing, 1997.

(9)   *Earth's Climatic History: The Last 1000 Years*, Center for the Study of Carbon Dioxide and Climate Change, www.co2science.org/subject/other/clim_hist_1thousand.htm.

(10) Daly, J., *The 'Hockey Stick': A New Low in Climate Science*, November 12, 2000. See web site www.microtech.com/au/daly/hockey/hockey.htm.

(11) Sagan, C., *The Demon Haunted World*—Science as a Candle in the Dark, Ballantine Books, New York, NY, 1996.

(12) Fara, P., *Learning from the Past*. See the Global Warming Debate—The Report of the European Science and Environment Forum, edited by J. Emsley, Bourne Press Ltd, Bournemouth, Dorset, 1996.

(13) The circumpolar vortex is the major flow of the atmosphere from west to east around the Earth, mainly over the mid latitudes. The flow is never strictly circular around the pole, but exhibits wave like movements with ridges and troughs in the pattern.

(14) The thermo-haline circulation moves warm surface water, and hence energy from the tropics (via for example the Gulf Stream) to the North Atlantic. As this water cools and as the salt concentration gradually increases it ultimately sinks and returns south as a deep current. The term *conveyor belt* has been used, but this is an overly simplified analogy.

(15) Broecker, W., et al, *Possible 20th-Century Slowdown of Southern Ocean Deep Water Formation*, Science, **286**, November 5, 1999.

(16) Black, D., et al, *Eight Centuries of North Atlantic Ocean Atmosphere Variability*, Science, **286**, November 26, 1999.

(17) Baliunas, S., et al, *The Sun Also Warms*, presented at the GCMI/CEI Cooler Heads Coalition meeting, March 24, 2000. This George C. Marshall paper is also available at: www.marshall.org/sunalsowarms.htm.

(18) World Climate Report, *A High-Stick 100-Year Forecast*, March 5, 2001. See Web site: www.greeningearthsociety.org/climate/v6n12/hot1.htm.

(19) Additional references are incorporated into Blocks 2 and 3 of the text.

11. The Invasion of the Gorons-VI: North of the Border

Introduction

While the Gorons[1] had their fun over the EPA report[2]—the infamous Climate Action Report for 2002—and extracted a little bit of revenge, it has been short lived. The Bush Administration has so far persevered brilliantly. Three recent events highlight their current success.

- The Johannesburg meeting on Sustainable Development, also known as Rio + 10, turned into a huge defeat for the Gorons. The Rio Conference in 1992 was where all this global attention on sustainable development and climate change started. This was where Agenda 21 was born. And this was where the Framework Convention on Climate Change (FCCC) and the follow-up meetings for the Conferences of the Parties (COPs) was organized.

However, the Rio + 10 meeting saw the Kyoto Protocol(KP) essentially kept off the agenda and saw specific targets for renewable energy rejected. More importantly the focus for this meeting was more on fighting poverty, on developing adequate water supplies and adequate energy supplies. It was focused on the sustainable development of significant economic growth.

- The results of COP VIII, from India, where the Delhi Ministerial Declaration supported "a major shift of emphasis from energy suppression to economic development and adaptation[3]." This document "failed to compel poor countries to cut greenhouse gases[4]." India, speaking for the "Group of 77" undeveloped countries, "said the economic advancement of developing countries should not be checked in order to prevent global warming."
- The November, 2002, elections added the final humiliation. Those of the conservative persuasion rose to the situation with solid support and a great turnout. The results were as close to a rout as one had any hope of ever seeing. Now the Gorons were really mad. And they still are.

The Bush team surely was elated at the success of the election, and permitted themselves a modest celebration. However, they barely had time for this little victory party, when word reached Washington that the Gorons had opened up a new front in Canada. Today the city of Ottawa is full of these aliens, both inside and outside the government, eager to commit whatever mischief they can. And the focus of this mischief making would be primarily the global warming issue and the KP.

As noted earlier *there are aliens on Earth from neighboring planets in the Alpha Centauri system—namely planets Gore and More. It was mentioned that the Morons were present in some concentration, on the Florida battlefield, side by side with the Gorons. And now it would seem they are also present in Canada, and have also infiltrated the federal government to a major extent. These aliens are now conducting this new Canadian offensive through two divisions, namely the Moron Division and the Goron Division.* We will comment briefly on each of these.

The Moron Division: The Françoise Ducros Affair

The Moron division in Canada was headed by General Françoise. Known affectionately as Ferocious Françoise formerly of the French Foreign Legion (FFfFFL). For the sake of brevity, we will refer to her simply as FF. She clearly was a woman not to be messed with. Like General Patton, her reputation preceded her. Françoise Ducros has never admitted that she was or is a Moron, but indeed she is.

Now when one is an alien, either from planet Gore, or from planet More, or whatever, the tendency is to operate underground and to keep ones background hidden. As a result, few Americans in the State Department or in the Pentagon, knew of her as General Françoise. FF's day job was Director of Communications for Prime Minister Chrétien, head of the Canadian government. Unfortunately she has now lost that job over an international incident that has become known as The Françoise Ducros Affair.

It seems that Ferocious Françoise had one bad habit: she tended to see everyone she met as a fellow Moron. It has been reported that she frequently called her associates Morons, and may even have called Prime Minister Chrétien a Moron. Chrétien "joked that Ducros uses the word 'moron' regularly, probably even against him[5]." Hence it came as no surprise that she recently alleged that President Bush was really a Moron in disguise. So naturally she called him a Moron.

Initially Chrétien stood by his famous general, but as it became clear that she no longer could lead any future campaign—particularly the imminent ratification battle on the Kyoto Protocol—she had to step down. "'The story wouldn't die' so she fell on her sword[6]."

One thing the effort for the Kyoto Protocol could not stand would be a bunch of angry and agitated Morons, running all over the battlefield, without any effective leadership. It would be Florida all over again. So FF[7] had to go.

The Goron Division: The David Anderson File

While Albert Gore Jr. is known as the Head Goron (HG) in the United States, David Anderson is his counterpart in Canada. In this essay he will be referred to as the DA. Anderson is the Environmental Minister in the Chrétien administration. The DA is a lawyer by education and a career politician/bureaucrat by experience. He also has spent much time earning his *green* credentials, most of it in British Columbia. It would appear that the DA is even more green than the HG. His environmental highlights would include:

- From 1968 to 1972 he founded and chaired the Special Committee on Environmental Pollution.

- From 1975 to 1993 he was a law instructor and environmental consultant at the University of Victoria. He also worked with the British Columbia Wilderness Federation on wetlands protection and on marine pollution. He also served as an advisor to the Premier of British Columbia on tanker traffic and on oil spills.

- From 1993 to the present he has been a member of parliament for Victoria, served as Minister of Fisheries and Oceans, has negotiated the Pacific Salmon Treaty with the United States, and established Canada's first Marine Protected Areas. In 1999 he was appointed Minister of the Environment. In 2001, he became the first Canadian ever to be elected to be President of the Governing Council of UNEP[8].

This DA has been Chrétien's point man on the Kyoto Protocol for several years. In October he presented a draft implementation plan where industry would bear as much as 40% of the cost and consumers less than 10%. Naturally he did not bother himself with such details as that the industry would have to pass their added costs on to consumers. The provinces complained bitterly that "Ottawa has not produced a workable plan and that the economic cost of implementation will be too high[9]." The DA's response: "'We are dealing with Kyoto for future generations. We're dealing with it to minimize the impact of climate change on future generations in Canada and internationally'". The DA added: "'It's for our grandchildren, great grandchildren and generations beyond'". Sounds like something that would have come from the HG himself or even his ex boss. As to more current matters, no estimate of the actual costs to taxpayers or no breakdown of percent emission cuts by specific industry was provided. The DA indicated that these aspects would not be available before ratification.

In April, 2002 Chrétien indicated "the government hopes to ratify the KP on climate change 'one-day'[10]." This in spite of a letter, signed by all provinces ex Quebec, that "indicated almost unanimous provincial opposition to ratification[11]." Recently Chrétien has indicated he want's to ratify the Kyoto Protocol by the end of year, possibly before Christmas. The provinces have almost begged[12] for a first minister's conference on climate change, and presented their key principles as noted in the nearby box. While the DA welcomed this statement, indicating

> **Provincial/territorial governments inputs on Kyoto**
> - Canadians must have chance at full input into development of the plan.
> - Burden must be spread fairly. Costs and impacts must be clear, reasonable and achievable.
> - Provincial/territorial jurisdiction must be honored.
> - Real emission cuts since 1990 should be recognized.
> - No province/territory bear the financial risk involved.
> - Benefits from forest and agricultural sinks go to the province or territory owning the assets.
> - Other principles: Innovation and new technology must be supported; economic competitiveness of Canadian business must be maintained; Canada must continue to demand recognition of clean energy exports; and there must be incentives for shifting to green energy.

he could agree with much of it, he concluded by noting "We are absolutely and totally and firmly committed to two things. One the time-line of Kyoto and two, the target of Kyoto".

Various premiers have indicated they will continue to fight, even though they expect Chrétien will indeed get the ratification he so damnably wants.

- Premier Gordon Campbell of British Columbia did not rule out a legal challenge.

- Premier Roger Grimes of Newfoundland summarized the attitude of the provinces as "We'll be left with no option but to investigate every single way for us to resist any unilaterally imposed sanctions[13]." Grimes also said that "he can't understand why the federal government is so anxious to ratify a plan that is still at the draft stage." He noted that Chrétien's "hasty approach is unusual for a leader known for his patient approach to national issues." My suspicion is that Chrétien has been convinced by his advisors in general and the DA in particular that this is an issue on which he can make his own legacy, and help the Liberal Party retain power.

- Finally Premier Ralph Klein of Alberta, the number one critic of the Kyoto Protocol, "is holding out hope that Canada's next prime minister will scuttle the climate change agreement[14]." The federal government must hold elections by 2004, which could see a change in the support for this protocol at the federal level. Klein also noted "that Canada has until 2005 to rescind it's decision".

The Propaganda Campaign: The David Suzuki Brief

Invasions inevitably include a propaganda campaign, and, while not widely reported, there is little doubt that the Minister of Propaganda for the Goron/Moron axis in Canada, is one David Suzuki.

This writer would argue that Canada and the United States and a few other countries are under the most intense, creative, crafty and expensive propaganda campaign ever conducted in our world. It was noted earlier that the campaign launched by Goebbels[15], over World War II, literally pales in comparison. As also noted earlier, what I am doing here is stealing a technique frequently used by the liberals in equating their opponents to the Nazis. Ann Coulter[16], as noted in Chapter 1, commented on the regularity that conservatives are compared to the Nazis.

David Suzuki has a PhD in Zoology from the University of Chicago (1961). Since 1969 he has been a full professor at the University of British Columbia(UBC) in Vancouver and is with the Sustainable Development Research Institute at UBC. The author of more than 30 books and the creator/broadcaster of hundreds of TV/Radio shows, Suzuki is recognized as a world leader in sustainable development. He is the creator and driving force behind The David Suzuki Foundation and web site, aimed at promoting sustainable development. With this set of credentials, it will be rather difficult to criticize this scientist, let alone to make the case that he is the Minister of Propaganda for the Goron/Moron axis. I will start with fear mongering and close with sustainable development.

Table 1. Selected Quotations that Paint David Suzuki as a Fear Monger

Writer	Date	Source	Quotation
Terrence Corcoran	12.26.98	*Global Warming: The Real Agenda*, Financial Post.	Suzuki says global warming 'is the most urgent slow - motion catastrophe facing human-kind'.
Linda Jones	10.20.99	*The Science and Politics of Global Warming*, The Fraser Institute	Suzuki - - in the book: *It's a Matter of Survival*, depicts a warmer world in 2040: forests will disappear, fisheries will be affected, and there will be widespread starvation. The majority of the population in Canada's largest cities will be 'living in shanty-town slums' - - and an estimated 2 to 3 million will be 'roaming the country, searching for food and shelter'.
David Suzuki	08.21.02	*We all depend on nature*, CNews Science	Driving an SUV in the city, driving five blocks instead of walking or buying fresh strawberries or tomatoes in winter all have repercussions for weather and climate around the world
Linda Jones	05.09.99	*Environmental Guilt Unwarranted*, The Fraser Institute.	This report had a longer list: giving up exotic imported goods such as coffee, bananas, oranges and watermelons. If we don't, 'the consequences could be devastating'.
Chris Webden	09.27.02	*Suzuki says go green or go home*, The Gazette Online, U of Western Ontario.	According to Suzuki, human beings are taking too much from the environment and putting too many toxins and pollutants back in us 'We don't have the foresight to see the long term effects of our actions on the environment' Suzuki said, blaming the capitalist approach to - - -. Right now we are producing harmful carbon dioxide 30 percent faster than plants can consume it.
Thomas Gale Moore	11.20.01	*Health & Economics*, World Climate Report, V4, N18.	Study by the Suzuki Foundation, *Taking Our Breath Away*, finds that 16,000 Canadians die per year from air pollution and global warming.

(1) Fear Mongering. Glassman and Baliunas coined the word *calamitologists* as follows: "But in the view of the people we call 'calamitologists' it is man—especially modern man—who despoils nature, stomping around in the Garden of Eden, killing rare species, dumping slop in the streams, and, in a final flourish, turning this beautiful planet into an oven[17]." This surely seems to be a pretty good description of Suzuki as a 'calamitologist' or as a fear monger. Some direct quotes or reports in Table 1 reinforce this conclusion.

These citations paint a rather bleak present, and an even bleaker future, if true. I see no science in these, simply opinion. They do not describe the planet that I know. It would seem to me these more than amply qualify Suzuki to be classified as a fear monger.

(2) Sustainable Development (SD).

Another way to critique David Suzuki is to critique sustainable development And surely this has been done, with the very best on *eco-logic on-line*. The citations in Table 2 are from *eco-logic Powerhouse on-line*. If one can show that SD is unrealistic, even ridiculous, with a covert and socialistic agenda, then one has also shown David Suzuki to be essentially the same. Based on these inputs it would appear that SD meets the unrealistic and ridiculous tests. More importantly these inputs also surely have the covert and socialistic agenda written all over them.

The above arguments are why I see David Suzuki—and his foundation, located in Vancouver and continually producing beautiful, colorful, very professional looking feel-good items: reports, books, classroom aids, TV and radio programs etc, etc, etc—is essentially the Minister of Propaganda for the invasion by the Gorons/Morons in Canada. There is also some evidence[18] that Suzuki has a direct pipeline to Chrétien and his DA. This news item claimed that on a recent trip to Australia, and while being interviewed by the Australian Broadcasting Company it was indicated by the host that the Prime Minister Chrétien of Canada had attempted to contact Suzuki.

Unfortunately Suzuki and his foundation are now global in scope, eager to carry on their *mission* all over this planet.

Conclusions

Table 2 Comments on the Impracticality of So-Called Sustainable Development

Author	Date	Source	Quotation
Dave Skinner	12.02.00	*Better than Sex*, eco-logic on-line	One definition of SD indicates key targets are 'zero' climate damage, species extinction, soil damage, waste and pollution; improvement of resource use efficiency by a factor of 10; and, after 75% of the land base has been set aside 'for nature', zero human encroachment on that land. Increases in the 'manipulation or harvesting of nature' are to be forbidden, as are 'increases in concentrations in nature of substances that come from the earth's crust - - -'.
Henry Lamb	01.02.01	*What's wrong with Sustainable Development*, eco-logic on-line	UN has already defined what is unsustainable: high meat intake; frozen and convenience foods; fossil fuels; appliances, air conditioning; and suburban housing. SD is all about 'reducing or eliminating' these 'patterns of unsustainable production and consumption' and to re-educate the public to believe that this life-style change is necessary to protect the planet from biological devastation.
Henry Lamb	08.02.01	*Sustainable Development is not Sustainable*, eco-logic on-line.	The instruction book for SD, Agenda 21, stems from the 1992 Rio Conference on SD. One of the bastards sired by this effort was the concept for 'Smart Growth' in order to create 'sustainable communities'. This is a pathway to a collectivist state. The flaw in the concept of SD is the loss of the principles of freedom.

While the Republicans won big-time in the November, 2002 elections, the threat from the Gorons/Morons remain. Hence, the struggle is not over—on the role of government in general, and on the fate of the global warming issue in particular—and further battles, such as the battle now occurring in Canada, are inevitable. It is highly likely that the Gorons/Morons will win the immediate offensive, but with all the provincial/territorial governments, except Quebec, opposed to this pathway, the Canadian Liberal Party may be creating their own downfall over the long haul.

The ultimate victor in this global battle will be that side that can win the public relations campaign. The Invasion of the Gorons/Morons has entered that phase.

References and Notes

(1) Parts of this essay were first published at *eco-logic on-line*, December 15, 2002.

(2) The EPA Climate Action Report for 2002 is available at: www.epa.gov/globalwarming/publications/car/index.html.

(3) Ebell, Myron, *Climate change report from Delhi, eco-logic on-line*, November 15, 2002.

(4) *Climate meeting ignores targets plea*, BBC News, November 1, 2002.

(5) *Calls Bush 'Moron,' Keeps Job*, Newsday.com, November 23, 2002.

(6) Delacourt, Susan, *'The Story wouldn't die,' so she fell on her sword*, National Post, November 27, 2002.

(7) Let me make a confession and an apology. I do not know if Ms Ducros was ever a member of the French Foreign Legion. In fact I do not know her at all. She may be very intelligent and competent and accomplished much. All I know about is her recent foul-up. Next the apology: I am sorry for taking advantage of this foul-up. I couldn't resist using it to help start this essay. Ms Ducros, I wish you well and hope you can move on to something more enjoyable and fruitful.

(8) UNEP—United Nations Environmental Program. This UN office, along with the WMO—The World Meteorological Organization, are the joint sponsors of the IPCC the Intergovernmental Panel on Climate Change.

(9) *Anderson defends Kyoto plan*, The Globe and Mail, October 27, 2002.

(10) Toulin Alan, Canada: Will ratify Kyoto 'one day' Chretien says", National Post, April 16, 2002.

(11) *Focus on Climate Change—Where we are now*, Canadian Ecumenical Justice Initiatives, April to June 2002.
See: www.kairoscanada.org/english/programme/climateupdate.htm.

(12) Fraser, Graham, *Provinces in 12-point consensus on Kyoto. Ottawa will ratify climate change protocol, they say*, Toronto Star, October 29, 2002.

(13) Meissner, Dirk, *Premiers will fight Chretien's Kyoto plan, says B.C. premier*, and *Angry Newfoundland premier demands first ministers meeting on Kyoto*, Yahoo! News, October 29, 2002.

(14) Singer, S. Fred, *Canada likely to ratify Kyoto. Alberta may have last word*, The Week That Was, November 30, 2002.

(15) Reimann, Victor, *Goebbels*, Doubleday & Company, Inc., Garden City, New York, 1976.

(16) Coulter, Ann, *Slander—Liberal Lies About the American Right*, Crown Publishers, New York, NY, 2002

(17) Glassman, J. and Baliunas, Sallie, *Bush is Right on Global Warming*, AEI, 06.01. See: www.aei.org/oti/oti13068.htm.

(18) Daly, John, *His Masters Voice*, Still Waiting for the Greenhouse, November 2, 2002. See: www.vision.net.au/~daly/.

12. The Invasion of the Gorons-VII: The Kerry Enigma

Introduction to the Gorons in the Senate

It is, unfortunately, time for a new warning on the Gorons. Several prior reports have increased readers awareness of this alien group, and to the threat they represent. And indeed I have written briefly about the Gorons in the senate before, on Tom Daschle. Now another senator has emerged from the pits of the leftist senate. It is time to expose him to the public for what he is, if we can figure out what that might be.

The Gorons are one of the fastest growing alien groups[1] on this planet. How these Gorons reproduce is not totally known. Surely one of the more fertile nesting areas has been on the left side of the U. S. Senate. Perhaps it should come as no surprise, but this site has been a source of *out of control* biological activity for years. Indeed it has become the world's capital for flatulence production.

Now before one gets all upset that I am taking this analysis to such a low level, one should realize that one definition for flatulence is: *pompously embellished language*[2a]. Talk about a bulls-eye! There is so much evidence of *pompously embellished language* on the left that one doesn't know where to begin.

GOP take notice. What follows is a political opportunity, namely: **produce a CD or cassette** that captures all the infamous speeches from this crowd. Better make that a few of the infamous speeches from this crowd, and each heavily edited, as they do tend to get a bit lengthy. Now one would have to admit they have some oratorical superstars: Robert Bird, Barbara Boxer, Hillary Clinton, Tom Daschle, Tom Harkins, Ted Kennedy, Chuck Schumer and so forth. Who did I leave out? One could add in the former President of the Senate, Albert Gore Jr., also known as the Head Goron(HG), and he could even bring along his disciple from the recent Democratic Primaries, Howard Dean. Such a recording surely would win a *goldie* in the *pompously embellished language* category.

While this above group of politicians are oratorical superstars they are also flatulence[2b] superstars. Start with the senior balloon[3] from Massachusetts, clearly their leader (in flatulence production). Some can find socially redeemable aspects in him. I can't. I can't stand to listen to him or to watch him. I can't change channels fast enough or hit the off switch. The HG evokes the same reaction. It is a testimony as to what the Democratic Party has become that such individuals can be considered leaders of, and spokespersons for, that party.

I could go on and on, but I think I have made my point: primordial ooze has been created in the Senate. And out of that primordial ooze via the wonders of fantastic fermentation or whatever, has emerged many a new Goron. For those who think that I am jesting here, for those who think what I am suggesting is impossible, I would refer you to a recent news report where "workers in knee-high rubber boots slosh in the buildings two vast reflecting pools, vacuuming up great green gobs of goo[4]." OK, so the reference I'm citing is really for the state capital of Hawaii, but it does set some sort of precedent. And it may just tell one the origins of many of the senate Gorons.

The latest Goron emerging from this pit comes with the same initials as *JFK* namely John Forbes Kerry. Many of you will recall that Senator Bentsen, (another Democrat from a different time and perhaps a different planet) once said "Senator I served with Jack Kennedy. I knew Jack Kennedy. Jack Kennedy was a friend of mine. Senator, you're no Jack Kennedy[5]." This quote was not addressed to John F. Kerry, but it would seem to fit perfectly. Recently Kerry has toned down his efforts to recast himself in the image of *JFK*. In contrast since it conveys such an important aspect of Kerry, I will continue to periodically refer to him as JFK*. Also, **GOP** take notice again, this time for a bumper sticker such as: JFK*—**Would you want an asterisk as your president?**

In any event his search goes on for his true identity. He is looking everywhere. Perhaps the reason he has emerged as a flip-flopper is that he doesn't know who he is. Some have even asked the question[6] if he is a Democrat. Who is JFK* and what does it mean for the future of our country? That will be the objective of this essay.

The Vietnam Connection—the Military Record.

Kerry enlisted in the Navy in February of 1966, and was honorably discharged in January of 1970, essentially after four years of service. Part of this was on a guided missile frigate in the Pacific, and part as a commander of a *Swift* Boat, used on the Vietnam rivers. Kerry's military service was dangerous, and he was and is a decorated veteran, with three Purple Hearts, one Bronze Star and one Silver Star.

The Vietnam Connection—the Post Military Record—the 1970s.

In any form of enterprise—corporate, military or private activities—there are two key questions to ask and to answer, namely *the what*, and *the how* questions. The *what should I do* question is key in defining involvement and direction and commitment. The *how should I do it* question is of equal importance.

Recently, on the Iraq War, Kerry has been very critical on *the How* to question. On the *What question*, his differences with George W. Bush seems to have narrowed. In contrast he argues that on the *How to* question there are huge differences. He claims he knows how to do this endeavor the right way and George W. Bush does not. He has literally presented himself as Americas expert on *How to* do things. However, never in the annals of recorded history, has anyone failed so miserably on the *How to* question as he did on how to protest the Vietnam War.

Now Kerry had every right to protest the Vietnam war when he came home, and after his discharge. That was his answer to the *What should I do now* question. His answer to the *How should I protest that war* is what is at stake here. His methods, and his defense of his methods, include many examples of stupid and gullible behavior, of deception and dishonesty and of terrible judgement. Consider the following inputs.

(1) <u>Joined Vietnam Veterans Against the War (VVAW)</u> in 1970, a few months after his discharge. Many believed he joined to use the VVAW to boost his election odds in the 1970 and 1972 congressional races. Ultimately resigned membership in November 1971, after becoming one of its leaders and spokesperson.

(2) <u>He arranged</u>[7] for a private meeting with the Vietnamese emissaries in Paris, including their spokeswoman—Nguyen Thi Binh. However this visit and this discussion[8a, 8b] with Madame Binh was illegal.

(3) <u>He later criticized</u>[7] President Nixon for not accepting Madame Binh's assurances that the Vietnamese would release American prisoners if the U. S. troops simply left.

(4) <u>He helped organize</u>[7] and raise money for the protest meeting in DC, April 18-23, 1971, where veterans threw away their medals. He either threw away his own medals or ribbons, and the medals of other veterans in this protest.

He now claims he only threw away his ribbons, as if that makes any difference.

(5) On Earth Day, April 22, 1971, he testified[9] to the Senate Foreign Relations committee that soldiers, on a day to day basis, tortured, raped, killed and mutilated women and children. But his testimony was based on hearsay, and it essentially impugned every one who fought over there.

(6) He wrote a book entitled *The New Soldier*, with the cover showing a group of bearded vets holding the American flag upside down. This highly controversial book[10] is essentially a photo essay of a 1971 anti-war protest. It is almost impossible to find a copy today. Could the Kerry campaign be striving to lock up all copies of this book? I would suggest that his behavior is closer to aiding and abetting the enemy, rather than the text book answer on *how to* do something.

The Vietnam Connection—the Contemporary Vietnam Connection.

Kerry's connection to Vietnam does not end with the medal/ribbon incident. In spite of his disgraceful protest in the 1970s, Kerry seems to have emerged as the authority on that country. Three areas are reviewed briefly where Kerry has had an involvement, and each of these comes with its own unique controversy.

(1) Agent Orange. In 1990 Kerry sponsored legislation to compensate Vietnam veterans for Agent Orange exposure. Kerry made the basis of this legislation that "it is not only appropriate, but scientifically correct." In short, their basis for compensation was "a supposed definite scientific link…that didn't and still doesn't exist…rather than a moral duty which does." Today, thanks to those "who established by declaration the notion that Agent Orange caused health problems, it will be difficult to rationalize why Vietnam vets are compensated for Agent Orange exposure, but Vietnam citizens shouldn't be[11]."

(2) POW/MIA. In 1992 Kerry was frocked as "Chairman of the Senate Select Committee on POW/MIA (Priosners of War/Missing in Action) Affairs." Their 500 page report concluded there were no longer any POW alive in Vietnam. Many POW/MIA families did not believe this report and found their agenda as one of "racing to normalize relations with Vietnam[12]." Further there was a hint of a deal with Colliers International, where the CEO was a Kerry cousin, and who won a major contract with Vietnam.

(3) Christian Repressions. In 2004 several reports[13, 14] have indicated that hundreds of Montagnard Christians have been slaughtered this year by the Vietnam military. Such an action would demand a response by the U. S. Government, but it has been reported that such a response has been held up by Kerry!

Domestic Policy.

Domestic Policy—Energy.

Kerry, using an Earth-Day[15] stop in Houston, complained about the administrations management of energy and the environment. Of course, he alleged the current gasoline price increase was due to President Bush's friendship with oil producing countries. Not only is this charge insulting, but it completely ignores the situation on OPEC supply and politics: for example, does Kerry want us to tell Saudi Arabia to produce more or else? Or else what—we will bomb? Isn't it likely that the Al Qaeda are now telling Saudi Arabia exactly the opposite, to produce less or we, the Al Qaeda, will bomb?

It also completely ignores the situation with, and the condition of, our refineries: dozens of different gasoline blends mandated by the government; no new refineries for years; and no passage of the Administrations energy plan, that would have included some modest relief on both domestic oil supplies and on refining regulations.

Part of this plan would be drilling and production from ANWR (Arctic National Wildlife Refuge). The Gorons have repeatedly argued that there is not enough oil there to justify *despoiling* this pristine refuge. First of all when Gorons use the word pristine, be very suspicious. Secondly, only a tiny fraction of the land will be utilized, such as 0.005 percent. That is five one thousandth of one percent. And finally the size of the oil reserve has been estimated at around 10 billion barrels, representing a value, at current prices, of $400 billion. No other country in the world is going to allow such a reserve to go untapped. Expected production rates of about one MBPD have been suggested. Compare this with Kerry's goal of two MBPD reduction in oil imports. Hence utilization of ANWR output would be a big step towards achieving that goal. Clearly producing from the ANWR reserve is important. And so is energy conservation. There is nothing wrong with energy conservation, but we should do both.

Back to the current gasoline price. Kerry charges that Americans will pay an additional $24 billion for gasoline. This current concern on the cost to motorists also conveniently ignores the fact that about ten years ago Kerry proposed[16] a 50 cent per gallon gasoline tax—a tax that would have added about $50 billion to the annual cost of gasoline. Amongst other things this suggests that Kerry is a just little bit of a hypocrite.

While Kerry continues to carp on the current gasoline price his campaign web site outlines a program focusing on conservation, alternative fuels, and on inventing our way out of this situation. All of his proposals are not new and many have been proposed by the Bush administration. However one aspect that is sort of new, or at least rejuvenated, is the use of the phrase: *energy independence.* Haven't heard about this idea since the days of Nixon, Ford and Carter and Project Independence.

A Kerry spokesman[17] charged the Bush Administration is trying to mislead Americans about how hard it will be to meet oil independence. I would counter that the Kerry team is trying to mislead Americans about how easy it will be to meet oil independence. Consider some specifics from their energy plan[18] that illustrates some of the simplicity, duplicity and hypocrisy involved

(1) <u>CAFE Standards.</u> In 2002 Kerry proposed that we boost the CAFE (Corporate Average Fuel Economy) from about 24 miles per gallon (mpg) to 35 mpg by 2015, almost a 50 percent increase. In his more recent energy plan he states that "Americans should drive the cars, SUVs, minivans and trucks of their choice, but these can be safer, more efficient and affordable[19]." Yet to get to 35 mpg auto makers will need to make the vehicles smaller and lighter—not the pathway to increased safety; and/or more complex such as the electric or hybrid—not the road to affordable vehicles.

(2) <u>Hydrogen Use</u>. Kerry proposes that this fuel be used throughout the nation by 2020. However he doesn't say what market share should be met by 2020. Clearly there is a huge difference between one percent and 99 percent. To his credit Kerry acknowledges that the Hydrogen has to be produced. Most Gorons completely ignore this requirement. Kerry suggests this can come from natural gas or coal. But supply of natural gas is already very tight, and adding a big incremental demand for auto use could send the price out of sight. This will also lead to much more investment in LNG terminals and/or coal gasification—options the Gorons are sure to scream at.

(3) <u>Renewable Energy</u>. Kerry proposes a goal of 20 percent of electricity from renewable energy by 2020. This sounds very noble, but the devil is in the details. California, for example, essentially focused its energy plan of the 1990s on wind energy, and major problems occurred. California built about 15,000 large wind mills, truly a massive commitment to wind energy. While there contribution to it's electrical supply was and is significant, the amount is still tiny, a little over one percent of total state generation. Further, since this energy is available only about 18 percent of the time, additional power generation capacity is still needed to back up this source, or the over all reliability of the system falls.

As a nation we need to be very careful we don't do what California has done, as noted in Chapter 5. For example their naive support for wind mills, along with massive constraints on conventional energy systems, and along with a terribly designed *deregulation* scheme, led to an operating and financial nightmare, including a situation where corporate shysters, in the guise of energy traders, came in *and picked the bones clean.*

Domestic Policy—Climate Change.

Considering the importance of the Iraq situation, the global warming issue has received little attention of late. Yet there is little question that it will be a major focus of any Kerry administration. A little more than a year ago Kerry was defining global warming as the biggest threat since the emergence of the cold war in the late 1940s. And just as we needed to invest heavy to build up our defenses against communism then, so today we need to invest heavy to build up our defenses against radical Islamism. Only he didn't say that. What he said was that we needed to invest heavy to build up our defenses against the "threat, obviously, of global warming[20]." Obviously? Maybe that was the position of Al Gore[21] as he gave "a completely paranoid speech, in 2004, about global warming, when the temperature was 22 [degrees] below normal." Kerry and Gore are in the same league on disinformation. Indeed Kerry might be even "Gorier than Gore on Global Warming", if that were possible.

So what is JFK*'s solution to this *terrifying threat*? While he might not have said precisely—I will go to the UN—that is essentially his position. In 2003 Kerry noted: "Bush's abrupt and unilateral decision to abandon discussions with the world community on climate change was early evidence of this administrations misguided approach to dealing with the community of nations. Dropping out of international implementation of the Kyoto Protocol was foolhardy then, and it is even more obviously foolhardy today[22]." Obviously? There is that word again.

Let us face it. Kerry loves the UN. After all, isn't it the World's Great Debating Society. Nothing more, nothing less. Except the cards are stacked ahead of time. The conclusion to any debate is already known. On global warming this means the Kyoto Treaty and massive greenhouse gas cuts by everyone, meaning by the United States.

On specifics it sounds very much like he would want to have expenditures for the global warming issue, plus the energy independence initiatve, to be very analogous to the funding involved in fighting the Cold War.

Domestic Policy—The Environment.

Time doesn't permit a detailed analysis of JFK*'s environmental plan. Suffice it to say it will be coupled with his energy independence and climate change efforts, wrapped up in huge spending programs.

There is one area in the environment field that deserves noting, namely his wife's foundations, and the organization they have created, namely the Tides Center of Pennsylvania. This is an organization that has funded many very far left wing environmental projects. The various Tides units will be revisited later in the Alternative Identities Section under the Marx/Lenin option.

Foreign Policy

Foreign Policy—Intelligence Funding

In 1971, during his run for congress, Kerry was quoted as saying "he would like to almost eliminate CIA activity[23]." He has also been reported to say that he "wanted troop dispersal throughout the world only at the direction of the United Nations."

As time passed his intelligence opposition[24] was constant, with a bit of back-filling utilized as events dictated.

(1) In 1994 he proposed and voted to cut $1 billion on FBI counter terrorism programs and for battlefield intelligence.

(2) In 1995 he proposed an intelligence budget cut of $300 million per year from FY1996 to FY2000.

(3) In 1997 he asked why our intelligence costs continues to grow exponentially, even though the Cold War is over.

(4) In 2001, immediately after 09/11, he bemoaned the lack of funding the intelligence function received. Figures.

Today he argues his votes were aimed at changing the culture of our intelligence gathering, particularly towards more human, and less technical reliance. As noted above—backfilling.

Foreign Policy—The Iraq War

After September 11th the Democrats agreed unanimously to support President Bush in the foreign policy arena. Any attacks had to be limited to domestic issues. That constraint didn't last long. President Bush "once imagined that the Sept. 11 terrorist attacks produced a bipartisan climate(7)...." Not any more. Indeed, Kerry promised[25] not to attack the President when the war began. It took Kerry less than a month to break this pledge.

On the Iraq war, *his how to do it wisdom* includes: "I will go to the UN[26]." Of course the Bush administration has already obtained a new resolution out of the Security Council, including a 15—0 vote. I suspect Kerry would still *go back* with much fanfare. What other steps he might take would likely include direct visits with Russia, Germany, and France to get a first hand view of their positions. While some Americans may be unhappy with the Bush plan, most Americans will know that "going to U. N. headquarters, visiting foreign capitals and promising lots of jaw-jaw is no plan at all." Note: we will have more to say on jaw-jaw a bit later.

What is Kerry's true position on this war? He voted "no on the Gulf War, Yes on the Iraq war, No on the $87 billion for reconstruction, and today he is advocating a firm Yes on finishing the job." I suspect it will be very difficult for Kerry to forget about the Vietnam war peace movement. Even a year ago the peace movement, against the Iraq war, was very strong. "The left's opposition to this war is pathetic on the argument. It is fueled by irrational passions, first the left's hatred of the United States, and second by its hostility to George Bush. This peace movement will live in infamy as the last refuge of scoundrels[27]." In spite of that indictment, it is hard to see how Kerry will walk away form his prior associations with peace movements. Sooner or later he would cut and run.

Alternative Identities

It is now time to address the key question of this essay: who is John Kerry? There is no question that he is a Goron. Risking a bit of redundancy, he may well be a "useful idiot" (see below). As for his basic identity you will see I have some unique ideas on this subject. However I must warn the readers that it still may not be possible to come up with a precise identification. Indeed one reporter has noted "that it may take extraterrestrial intelligence to figure out John Kerry[23]." I suppose that is what one should expect in order to decipher a decedent from planet Gore.

Eight identity candidates have emerged. Most involve the concept of reincarnation, a science which is not out of the question in an essay where primordial ooze, and fantastic fermentation have been noted. Even more difficult will be an assessment of where JFK*, the master flip-flopper, might take this country.

First, the candidates.

(1) <u>Lurch</u>. Let me start with the popular idea, that has been suggested by Rush Limbaugh, and others, namely that Kerry is the reincarnation of Lurch, of Adams Family fame. While the resemblance is certainly there, surely the Democratic nominee would be a bit more polished and sophisticated.

Poems by Langston Hughes, Communist

1. Lines from the poem: **Let America be America again.**

(This title has been reported as a slogan under consideration for the John Kerry campaign.)

Let America be America again.
Let it be the dream it used to be.
Let it be the pioneer on the plain
Seeking a home where he himself is free.
(America never was America to me.)

Let America be the dream the dreamers dreamed—
Let it be that great strong land of love
Where never kings connive nor tyrants scheme
That any man be crushed by one above.
(It never was America to me.)

O, let my land be a land where Liberty
Is crowned with no false patriotic wreath,
But opportunity is real, and life is free,
Equality is in the air we breathe.
(There's never been equality for me,
Nor freedom in this "homeland of the free.")

2. Lines from the poem: **Goodbye Christ**

Goodbye
Christ Jesus Lord God Jehovah,
Beat it on away from here now.

Make way for a new guy with no religion at all—
A real guy named
Marx Communist Lenin Peasant Stalin Worker ME.

(2) <u>Deep Throat</u>. A university group[28] claims they have unmasked Deep Throat. I am personally unconvinced. Now I am surprised that no one else has come up with this idea that John Kerry is really Deep Throat. The timing is right as he was discharged in January of 1970 and Watergate occurred in June of 1972. Kerry also has a very deep throat. And he undoubtedly had little or any empathy for Nixon. Hence the idea is sound. Further his own brother attempted to pull off a similar stunt[29] later that year.

(3) <u>Ho Chi Minh</u>. Could Kerry be an American version of a reincarnated Ho Chi Minh? As much as the Vietnamese love Kerry, it is very unlikely that they would welcome this option.

(4) <u>Charles de Gaulle</u>. Could Kerry be an updated model of Charles DeGaule? I think I am getting closer. Kerry has the same physique, arrogance and coldness that characterized De Gaulle. And Kerry surely has a deep love for the French. At least one other pundit has raised this question, noting that, "De Gaulle seeking the French Presidency struck a deal and evacuated Algeria[30]." It sounds like this pundit has concluded that, Kerry seeking the American Presidency will strike a deal and evacuate Iraq.

However it is, again, very unlikely that the French would embrace the idea that Kerry is a return of De Gaulle. In fact, based on their recent track record, they would undoubtedly veto it.

(5)   <u>Neville Chamberlain</u>. I think I am getting very close. And it is unlikely that the English would oppose our adoption of their former leader and appeaser.

Chamberlain was the son[31] of the most famous Liberal Radical of the late 19th century. His father had been a leader of the Liberal-Unionist party and then a colonial secretary in the conservative party. Like his father, Chamberlain started out as a Labour politician, but switched loyalties, and in time rose to become a conservative prime minister (1937—1940). Unlike his father, Chamberlain brought little passion or excitement to his work. He seemed to be a classic civil servant and his strengths seemed to be his concern for administrative minutiae.

It is unclear why he felt he could negotiate with Hitler. It may have "sprung from a passionate desire to avert the horror of war." It may have stemmed from the general arrogance of the British as depicted in the book[32] *The March of Follies*. Or it may be that he fancied himself as an negotiator, much like John Kerry does today. Hence Chamberlain attempted to negotiate with "the obsessed and erratic Adolf Hitler[33]." In September of 1938 Chamberlain traveled to Europe three times. He came back with a treaty and reported: "My friends…, a British Prime Minister has returned from Germany bringing peace with honour. I believe it is peace for our time…. Go home and get a nice quiet sleep[34]." I think you will all agree that last clause had a nice touch to it, one they would long remember as the bombs were falling and the rockets were dropping.

(6)   <u>Marx/Lenin</u>. This option is perhaps the most difficult one to assess. The first piece of evidence is Kerry's trip to Paris in 1970, and his willingness to meet with communist representatives, and then later to support their party line. While that was over 30 years ago, it is still very disturbing.

The next piece of evidence is that the Kerry campaign may well have adopted a slogan "Let America be America again" from a poem written by Langston Hughes. This might be OK except Hughes was a well known communist[35], a hater of Christianity, and a lover of V. I. Lenin. A few lines from that poem, and a second poem by Hughes, entitled *Goodbye Christ*, are shown in the nearby box.

One might observe that it appears that Kerry has some rather strange people he has supported or embraced.

Now admittedly the above item is a pretty thin connection to Marx/Lenin. Let me go on. The term "useful idiots" was coined by Lenin to describe those mindless people who would always find ways to justify whatever the Communists were doing. Several writers, including Mona Charon[36], have raised the question if Kerry's true identity is that of a "useful idiot". In his 20s Kerry saw his country as an outlaw nation. He joined the VVAW and associated[37] with one of it's leaders, Al Hubbard who was a member of the Communist Party USA, and liked to spell America with a k, that is: Amerika. While it is true that Kerry had a falling out with Hubbard, as best as I can tell, that was based on Hubbard falsifying his Vietnam experience, and not on his ideology.

One might still observe that Kerry has had some rather strange contacts in his past.

Again, the above item is a pretty thin connection to Marxist/Leninist philosophy, but let me go on a bit more. There is the matter of his wife, or more precisely her foundations and the Tides Center of Pennsylvania, along with her relationship with the original Tides Foundation and Tides Center of San Francisco. They appear to be, among other things, a charity laundering scheme. They provide a mechanism for those who want to donate, but don't want others to know where the money is ultimately used. Such people want the tax credit, and they want there donation to go to some pet, leftist project, but no publicity. And the Tides entities have funded many very far left wing activities and organizations. The director, Drummond Pike, is a well known west coast leftist activist. One web site reports that Drummond's message is: "I can hide any amount of money I want and you can't find it[38]."

They have a major relationship with the Pew Charitable Trusts. The name of leftist Ramsey Clark also appears on one web site. Some of the organizations they support have a Communist heritage and some have a couple to the extremist Islamic movement. They seem to be all over the map of leftist issues.

One might observe that it appears Mrs. Kerry has some rather unique associates. Clearly this couple with Mrs Kerry, and in turn any couple with John Kerry, deserves very careful scrutiny and assessment.

Again the above linkage is thin on any connection to Marx/Lenin. But Kerry is one of the most liberal of all senators, voting 96 percent of the time with Senator Kennedy in support of a "strong tax raising and government best[29]" platform. While it would be hard to believe that Kerry is a Marxist/Leninist, it would not be hard to believe that he is a socialist.

(7) Jaws. It has been reported that JFK loved the Bond books/movies and read/saw all of them. Hence it is a near certainty that JFK* also read/saw the complete set. In particular the movies: *The Spy Who Loved Me* and *Moonraker* featured a character named Jaws played by a rather huge Richard Kiel, complete with Chromium steel teeth. However it has been reported[39] that Kiel was really Kerry. And indeed Jaws looks very much like Kerry.

Now JFK* has a very long face and a very strong jaw. He must be as proud of his jaw as he is of his negotiating skills. Armed with that jaw, *and his experience as Jaws*, he is ready for combat, ready to do some jawboning. Perhaps this is why Kerry, who perceives himself an expert in jawboning, is amazed that others are not. For example he has repeatedly counseled President Bush to head to Saudi Arabia and jawbone the Saudis to do his bidding.

For those who would like to see Kerry in action, with his long face and strong jaw, I would refer you to the following cartoon[40]. The cartoon features include:

- JFK* on the podium, with a banner containing huge letters *J F K*, with the rest of his name in very tiny letters.
- Underneath the letters is a heading: *Core Messages*. #1 has a question mark. #2 and #3 are blank.
- His speech consists of two words: *Ask Not*.
- One member, in an audience of two, observes: *Still Needs Work*.
- The tiny stick-man, in the lower right corner, comments: *Profile in Porridge*.

(8) <u>JFK</u>. Earlier it was noted that JFK* has been backing away from the idea that he is the second coming of this former president. That would seem to be a simple election calculation. But deep in his heart I believe that he still thinks he is another JFK. So JFK still belongs on this list.

So there they are. Eight prime candidates. And after exhaustive research I can't truly eliminate any of them. I would invite, and welcome, further research on these eight options by any member of the audience. In any event I suspect each of these candidates is some how related to JFK* and each, in some way, have left their mark on him.

6. Conclusions

Now I personally don't believe that JFK* will be elected, unless the situation in the Middle East turns real sour. If that were the case what can we expect from Kerry as president. First, much more debate. JFK* reportedly told an MTV audience that his first response to another 9/11 like attack would certainly not be to flex our military muscle. "I would want to talk to them". Clearly he thinks he can out debate them. Next we would have more negotiations, and the UN would once again be on a pathway to the League of Nations II. Unfortunately for the United States we could ultimately see some level of appeasement, much like De

Gaulle's withdrawal from Algeria. And our word in international relations would become utterly meaningless. The west would gradually be forced out of the Middle East, and in time possibly even out of the Mediterranean.

On domestic issues we would also see Kerry's love for the UN extend to embrace their position on climate change, along with a never ending path of emissions reductions. And finally we could expect massive expenditures to once again chase the the global warming myth and the "Energy Independence" fairy tale. This term is "a cipher phase of American political speech, existing mainly to meet a public attitude for escape from a troubled world. Let's hope that we're not so feckless as to evade the real fight against terrorism in favor of a fantasy that all will be well if Congress is allowed to spend billions on a pork-barrel scheme to wean industrial society off hydrocarbons[41]."

All in all if JFK* were to be elected we would face a most sobering and frightening future. Let us pray that it does not come to pass.

References and Notes

(1) Parts of this essay were first published at eco-logic on-line, July 1, 2004.

(2a) hyperdictionary. See: www.hyperdictionary.com/search.aspx?define=Flatulence.

(2b) There are two definitions of flatulence. Either would seem to apply for this citation.

(3) The practice of calling Ted Kennedy the *Senior Balloon*, comes from the Laura Ingrahm show.

(4) Kayal, Michelle, *In a Sparkling State, Goo Fills the Symbolic Pools*, New York Times, May 30, 2004.

(5) Stengel, Richard, *Ninety Long Minutes in Omaha. The overprogrammed Quayle was a poor match for Bentsen*, 10.17.88. See: www.cnn.com/ALLPOLITICS/1996/analysis/back.time/9610/09/index.shtml.

(6) Cox, Judson, *Is John Kerry A Democrat?*, eco-logic on-line, May 1, 2004. See www.eco.freedom.org/20040501/cox.shtml.

(7) Halbfinger, David M., *Kerry Role in Antiwar Veterans Is Delicate issue in His Campaign, New York Times*, April 24, 2004.

(8a) Morano, Marc, *Kerry's Meeting with Communists Violated US Law*, Says Author, CNSNEWS.COM, May 20, 2004.

(8b) Corsi, Jerome R., *Kerry and the Paris Peace Talks*. See www.wintersoldier.com, May 17, 2004.

(9) Purdum, Todd S., *In '71 Antiwar Words, a Complex View of Kerry*, New York Times, February 28, 2004.

(10) Kerry, John F. and Thorne David, *The New Soldier*, Simon & Schuster, October 1, 1971.

(11) Milloy, Steven, *Has Kerry Helped Vietnam Sue over Agent Orange?*, Fox News, February 6, 2004.

(12) Eberhart, Dave, *Why Families Say Kerry Betrayed POWs and MIAs*, NewsMax.com, February 13, 2004.

(13) Staff, *Vietnamese government represses ethnic minority Christians*, BPNews, Southern Baptist Convention, April 20, 2004.

(14) Thibault, David, *Kerry, McCain Alleged to be 'Fast Friends' of Vietnamese Communists*, CNSNEWS.COM, May 20, 2004.

(15) Williams, John, *Kerry at UH rally tells Bush to get tough with oil producers*, Houston Chronicle, April, 23, 2004.

(16) Easterbrook, Gregg, *50 cent gas tax hike still has mileage*, Houston Chronicle, May 30, 2004.

(17) *Kerry urges energy independence in U. S.*, USA Today, May 23, 2004.

(18) *Energy Plan*, John Kerry President web site, undated.
See: http://www.johnkerry.com/issues/energy/plan.html.

(19) Yates, Brock, *Jungle John's Reality Check*, TCS, March 4, 2004.
See: http://www:techcentralstation.com/030404G.html

(20) Brown, Steve, *Kerry Calls 'Global Warming' Biggest Threat Since Cold War*, CNSNEWS.COM, May 1, 2003.

(21) Michaels, P., *Kerry: Gorier than Gore on Global Warming*, January 30, 2004.
http://www.cato.org/dailys/01-30-04.html.

(22) *Candidate Kerry on Kyoto and global warming*, Cooler Heads Coalition, April 14, 2004. See: http://www.globalwarming.org/article.php?uid=622.

(23) Pike, John, *The Many Faces of John Kerry (Part 1)*, Insight on the News, August 29, 2003.
See: http://www.insightmag.com/main.cfm?include=detail&storyid455076.

(24) Eberhart, Dave, *Kerry on the Record: Attacking U. S. Intelligence*, NewsMax.com, February 19, 2004.

(25) *John Kerry's Flip Flops*, April 16, 2004. The Boston Globe reported the no criticism pledge on March 11, 2003 and the breaking of this pledge on April 3, 2003.
See: http://www.freerepublic.com/focus/f-news/1119904/posts.

(26) Krauthammer, Charles, *Kerry's stance on Iraq war may cost him*, Houston Chronicle, April 23, 2004.

(27) Horowitz, David, *The War Has Refuted the Opposition*, Townhall.com, Apri; 4, 2003. See:
http://www.townhall,com/columnists/davidhorowitz/dh20030404.shtml.

(28) Gaines, Bill, et al, *Who is Deep Throat?*, University of Illinois Department of Journalism, April 23, 2003. There candidate is Fred Fielding, deputy counsel to former President, Richard Nixon.
See: http://deepthroatuncovered.com/story/.

(29) Pike, John, *The Many Faces of John Kerry (Part 2)*, Insight on the News, September 2, 2003. See:
http://www.insightmag.com/main.cfm?include=detail&storyid455080.

(30) *Is John Kerry Charles de Gaulle?*, WhiteDog, April 24, 2004. See:
http://whitedog.typepad.com/test_bed/2004/04/is_john_kerry_c.html.

(31) *Neville Chamberlain.* See http://www.grolier.com/wwii/wwii_chamber.html.

(32) Tuchman, Barbara W., *The March of Folly—From Troy to Vietnam*, GK Hall & Co., Boston, 1984. See Section Four.

(33) *Britain Goes to War*, April 18, 2003. See http://www.otr.com/newville.html.

(34) *Peace for Our Time by Neville Chamberlain.*
See http://www.lib.byu.edu/~rdh/eurodocs/uk/peace.html.

(35) Buckley Jr., William F., *A Campaign Slogan for Kerry"*, NRO, nationalreviewonline, June 2, 2004.
See: www.nationalreview.com/buckley/wfb200406021606.asp.

(36) Charon, Mona, *Useful Idiots—How liberals Got it Wrong in the Cold War ad Still Blame America* First, Regnery Publishing, Inc., Washington DC, 2003.

(37) Kincaid, Cliff, *Kerry's Commies Friends*, Media Monitor, Ma7 7, 2004.
See: http://www.aim.org/media_monitor_print/1497_0-2_0/.

(38) Drummond Pike—*Secrecy, pass-through, and lobbying guru for hundreds of left-wing groups and their founders*, Undue Influence, undated.
See: http://www.undueinfluences.com/drummond_pike.htm.

(39) Renzo's Rant—*John Kerry's Terrible Secret.*
See: http://www.angelfire.com/apes/renzorant/kerry.html.

(40) Toles, Tom, Cartoons, Washington Post, May 31, 2004. See:
http://www.washingtonpost.com/wp-dyn/opinion/tolestom/?name=Toles
&date=20040531.

(41) Jenkins Jr., Holman W., *Nothing to Say? Talk About 'Energy Independence'*, Wall Street Journal, June 2, 2004.

13. The Left Will Use Absolutely Anything: On Hype, Propaganda and Duplicity

Introduction

As I noted in the Preface, the bulk of the propaganda comes from the Left. The Democrats will, of course, argue the exact opposite. For example as I write this essay I had just listened to the early morning radio *debate* between John McCain and Ted Kennedy. McCain's input was that our presidential campaign had become so negative, and he asked Kennedy to join him in an appeal to the two candidates to take the positive road for the balance of the campaign. Kennedy responded that *all of this negative campaigning had originated from the Right. In contrast, Kerry has ran a very positive program*. Well not hardly. One example: the Left have out spent the Right ten to one on 527 advertisements. As noted in Chapter 12, I have zero respect for Ted Kennedy. I can't change channels fast enough when he comes on.

The Left Will Use Absolutely Anything.

Seldom has the Left been more egregious in the use of hype and distortion than with the following charge against the City of Houston, used during the 2000 presidential election. The Left became rather desperate and were looking for anything to throw at the then Texas governor, much as they are desperate today, during the 2004 election. Back in 2000 a Democrat spokesperson, Jennifer Lazlo-Mizrahi, amongst others, "launched an assault on the City of Houston saying 'we need to start letting people know, for example, that Houston is a *filthy, smoggy, disgusting city*'[(1)]." The basis for these charges was that Houston had replaced Los Angeles as the most polluted city in the country. If true the implication was that George W. Bush was responsible for this situation and guilty of being an anti-environmentalist. Some comments:

(1) **Hype**. The choice of the words *filthy and disgusting* surely qualify as hype. They don't describe the Houston that I know. Major areas of Houston are blessed with many grand, even spectacular trees. While not the Muir Woods of California, Houston is a part of the Great Piney Woods of the South. Indeed there are four national forests and one national preserve, The Big Thicket, north, and northeast of Houston. One could also note the abundance of *Live Oak* trees in this area, with their magnificent profile, reminiscent of the *spreading Chestnut tree*. One could also add the *Pin Oak* trees with their magnificent leaf, whose shape out performs the Canadian Maple Leaf. And one could also include the incredible *Crepe Myrtle* trees and shrubs, the *Lilacs* of the south, that are in bloom six months of the year, versus six days for their northern look a-likes.

See the next section for more comments on the natural resources of Houston.

(2) **Propaganda**. Here the Democrats were striving to paint George W. Bush as guilty of terrible environmental leadership and stewardship. Not only did they ignore the accomplishments of Texas over the past 10 to 20 years, but also ignored the fact that Bush, as governor of Texas, had zero responsibility and zero control over the Houston air quality in general, and any smog there in particular.

(3) **Duplicity**. If there was any one politician that had some responsibility and influence on this matter, it would have been the mayor of Houston, Lee P. Brown. A Democrat, his influence was that of the bully pulpit—as the EPA, and the state analog of the EPA, were in charge and monitored emission releases and air quality very carefully, and continued to push Houston forward on the one criteria pollutant, ozone, that was out of compliance—but nowhere was Browns name seen connected to this problem.

Where the Mayor's bully pulpit was needed was to defend the city from the unfair and scurrilous attacks coming from Washington and New York. This effort was needed, first to defend the city's image in general, and the resultant impact on such items as convention bookings, business relocations and overall tourism. It was also needed to protect the city's significant investment, in effort and in money, several million dollars, in pursuing the selection to be the U. S. candidate city for the 2012 Olympics. In such a competition the city could not afford a single black mark. Yet Mayor Brown did absolutely nothing, although he was one of the prime movers on the Olympic bid. His cohorts—in other democratic offices in Houston and in Washington—also did nothing to correct this situation. In a contest where image, and the perceived quality of life of each city, was going to be the dominant factor, these politicians did zero to refute these spurious charges.

This is Park Country.

It took Elyse Lanier, the wife of the former mayor, Bob Lanier, and chairwoman of the Houston Image Group, to set the record straight[2]. "Houston is an amazing city, with great museums, theaters, renowned colleges, family attractions…" She went on: "I know from personal experience that once we get people here to visit…they are pleasantly surprised. "They didn't know Houston was so green, had so many restaurants, theaters, museums and parks." A bit more: "Let me take you on a tour of my Houston where the azaleas have just finished a spectacular season and the roses are starting to bloom."People are jogging along the Bayou as we head downtown…." And finally: "We need to spread the real message about our great city. "Unfortunately it seems some of our messengers aren't up to the task".

The Buffalo Bayou deserves note. As Houston emerged from the homesteads of the early 1830s this tiny bayou was the artery of commerce, from the Gulf of Mexico/Galveston Bay right into what is now downtown Houston. Over the next 100 or so years, including World War II, it became the center of the petroleum refining and petrochemical industries of the United States. It was dredged extensively creating what is known as the Houston Ship Channel, bringing ocean going ships to within four miles of downtown. And it was polluted extensively. Environmentalists will argue that all of this was an unforgivable sin. Indeed if any of the polluters of this bayou were breaking the law at that time, then they surely should have been punished for that offense. However, the overall changes to the bayou, I would like to think, were part of the industrial growth process that has created the economic muscle of this country.

And with that success has now come a major drive to further clean up and improve this natural resource. East of downtown, San Jacinto State Park and Museum is a gem hidden amongst the distillation towers and oil tanks that prevail in that area. This park is a memorial to those who defeated Santa Ana in 1836. It also salutes the battleship USS Texas, and all who served on it, during World War I and World War II. Both the museum and the battleship are worth a visit. Suggestion: take Interstate 10 east of town, then the Lynchberg ferry exit (number 787) south. This route will avoid most of the refinery/petrochemical maze.

West of downtown this bayou is the home of several fine parks. First is Memorial Park, the *Central Park* of Houston. Others deserving mention include the Houston Arboretum, and a satellite facility of the Houston

Museum of Fine Arts—The Bayou Bend Collection and Gardens. In addition there are several golf courses, plus an urban park along the Bayou, that runs into and through the downtown area. This area also includes a large number of grand residential areas such as River Oaks. There are some who say that this enclave is the most important location in Houston. The not so hidden secret of this little island of wealth is that it is no where near any river. It is on the Bayou!

Although vastly improved over the past 20 years, additional areas for rejuvenation of the Bayou remain[3]. It soon will become as well known a resource to the Houston area, as the creeks and rivers of San Antonio, Dallas and Austin.

Conclusions.

If we set aside the comments from Jennifer Lazlo-Mizrahi, as that of a carping, political hack, one might ask if there is any substance to the charges that Houston had replaced Los Angeles as the most polluted city in the country. Well as it turns out, not very much. The basis for this claims is extremely thin, namely that

- for two years, and
- on only one out of six criteria pollutants—ozone—Houston barely exceeded LA. The reason for this *honor* was not any dramatic increase in the ozone levels or frequency of occurrences in Houston, but rather an amazing and commendable decline in these values for LA.

The above commentary is not to claim that there are no serious air pollution problems left in Houston. There are, and people are working on them. The purpose here, however, is to emphasize that the political hacks have not *shot square* with the American public on this issue. They have deliberately insulted and scarred a rather fine city, and one that is doing more than it's share to solve the energy problems of our country.

And if the Left is not shooting square, on this issue—if they will use anything, say anything and do anything to try to make their point—one has to wonder what are the other issues where they behave the same?

References and Notes.

(1) Levin, Marc, *Democratic Spokesman Says "Houston is Filthy"*, Houston Review, September/October 2000. See: www.houstonreview.com/articles/FilthyHouston.html.

(2) Lanier, Elyse, *It would help if Houstonians stopped selling our city short*, Houston Chronicle, April 8, 2001.

(3) Snyder, Mike, *A better Bayou*, Houston Chronicle, September 22, 2002.

14. Conclusions: Why I am a Skeptic on the Global Warming Issue

Introduction.

There have been hundreds of reports expressing concern on global warming, putting pressure on the United States and Canada to support the Kyoto Protocol (KP). These reports bear such lineage as the United Nations, the prestigious British magazine *Nature*, the U. S. Magazine *Science*, and such news magazines as *Time*. With this flood of support how can one be skeptical on this issue? Count me on the skeptics side[1].

While the number of skeptics has been reported as small, one petition[2] has been signed by about 20,000 scientists, engineers and others. As noted in Chapter 3 most skeptics are well informed with some coming across as positive, brilliant, and human, far from the mediocre scientists that they are frequently called.

Skeptics have been ridiculed. Such attacks are inconsistent with the National Academy of Sciences code of conduct, which indicates that "the fallibility of methods is a valuable reminder of the importance of skepticism in science. Scientific knowledge...must be continually scrutinized for possible errors." The code goes on: "a searching skepticism as well as an openness to new ideas are essential to guard against intrusion of dogma or collective bias into scientific results." Unfortunately we are very close to this condition today.

Key Assumptions.

There are four key assumptions on the global warming issue:

(1) **Our planet is warming.** Detection of warming is hard. Clearly there is no single, non-controversial spot, where one could insert a high quality thermometer, and get the answer.

Elaborate surface temperature databases have been assembled with data from thousands of weather stations around the world. However, these stations lack identical instrumentation and station setting and environment. Further, far more of their measurements are based on land, far more of their measurements are in the northern hemisphere, and far more of their measurements are in developed areas, where *urban heat-island effects* are a factor. Hence, the distribution of stations is far from uniform, and coverage is far from complete. Based on such databases, globally averaged temperature is about 0.6°C warmer today versus 100 years ago.

As an alternative approach to surface databases, a database of temperatures measured from satellites has emerged. While only 23 years old, it's coverage of our planet is 100%, and far more uniform. This database shows there has been only a tiny, if any, warming over its history.

Hence, there is a significant debate over whether global warming has been detected or not.

(2) **This warming is caused by society.** The proponents of this issue automatically assume society is guilty. But there are as many, if not more reasons to point to Mother Nature. We, on planet Earth, live in an ocean of cyclical phenomena. The daily and annual cycles are the most obvious. Other cycles include the ill-defined 2–7 year El Nino events, the 11 year sunspot cycle, longer solar cycles of 80 to 1500 years, and very long term cycles of 19,000 to 100,000 years. While our understanding of these cycles is embryonic, it is rapidly improving, including a start of understanding of their couple to climate. Hence finding society guilty today is surely premature.

Proponents rely on computer models to make their case, the so-called GCMs. What is frequently ignored or left unpublicized is the quality of these models. Dr. William Gray, the leading hurricane forecaster from Colorado State University, has been most outspoken in this area. In a 1997 Houston speech he commented: "when modelers move out onto the climate area, the complexity becomes too damn much[3]."

For over ten years Dr. Richard Lindzen, the Sloan Professor of Meteorology at MIT, has been the leading critic of these models. His concerns include what he considers inappropriate treatment of water vapor and cloud cover. For example, these models only predict a significant warming when a water vapor feedback mechanism is incorporated. Yet the physics of this feedback[4] is essentially unknown. Without this feedback, the increased levels of carbon dioxide will not lead to the dramatic warming predicted.

(3) **This warming will be catastrophic.** Well not likely. First of all there will be benefits such as lower fuel bills, increased crop yields and increased forest growth.

Secondly, climate history over the past 1200 years, as noted in Chapter 10, would suggest that a warming period is not all that bad, whereas a cooling period is the one to be concerned about.

Finally the proponents, according to Dr. Stephen Schneider[5], of Stanford "have to offer up scary scenarios, make simplified, dramatic statements, and make little mention of any doubts we might have." He went on: "Each of us has to decide what the right balance is between being effective and being honest." Surely this is what Time magazine[6] is doing when it shows a picture of planet Earth, in a frying pan, on it's cover.

(4) **Society knows what to do to prevent this warming.** Well not likely. For example Dr. James Hansen of NASA, in 1988, became the *father* of this issue, with his testimony before congress that society-caused global warming was essentially here. But in 1998 he confessed that "the *forcings* that drive long term climate change are not known with an accuracy sufficient to define future climate change[7]." Based on this confession we **should close this issue down** or at least put it on hold for 10 to 20 years.

Another example is Dr. Tom Wigley of the National Center for Atmospheric Research. He published the results from his latest computer runs in 1998, again as noted in Chapter 3, and found the KP, if fully implemented by all involved nations by 2010—an event that would seem impossible to achieve—would reduce warming 0.07°C by 2050, and another 0.13°C by 2100. These amounts are so minuscule as to be unmeasurable. This means societies are being asked to spend trillions, on a course of action that we won't know is ever doing any good.

Further, assuming the *warmers* science is valid, we would have to implement not just one KP, but **about 15 successive emission cuts** to prevent a warming of say 3°C (assume 0.2°C per cut times 15 cuts). But what is debated today is just the first cut. No mention is made of any subsequent cuts required. Yet all the countries involved would have a terrible, if not impossible task, in meeting the first KP cuts alone.

Conclusions.

All of the four critical assumptions have been assessed and found to be rather questionable. None of them can be said to have been definitively confirmed to date. It is clear that the science behind global warming is complex and incomplete. But the consequences of starting down the KP pathway are so enormous that it benefits us all to make sure we get the science right and not settle for a politically defined solution, which is what the KP is all about. The KP would cost the North American taxpayer trillions of dollars, dramatically affecting our economies, with no assurance this investment would solve any problem.

It is my conviction that the proponents of this issue have not proven carbon dioxide guilty. Even more so they have not made the case that it is imperative we act immediately.

I do not see the catastrophic future painted by the proponents of the KP. It is far easier to see serious economic hard times if society constrains itself any further than it already has on nuclear power, that it has considered doing on hydro power, and that it would do on fossil fuels if caps were placed on carbon dioxide emissions.

Hence I do not support the Kyoto Protocol which I believe is terribly flawed and possibly even fraudulent.

References and Notes

(1) Earlier versions of this essay were first published in:
* * The Houston Chronicle, June 17, 2001, with Michael T. Halbouty, and
* * The Austin Review, November 6, 2001, with Michael T. Halbouty, and
* * The Green & White, University of Saskatchewan Alumni Association, Fall 2002.

(2) See Chapter 10, Note 6c.

(3) Gray, W., Colorado State University, *Predicted Hurricane Activity for 1997: Is Global Warming Causing More and Bigger Hurricanes?*, Speech at the National Hurricane Association meeting, Houston, TX, April 25, 1997.

(4) Lindzen, Richard S., *The Origin and Nature of the Alleged Scientific Consensus*, Regulation, The Cato Review of Business & Government, Spring 1992.
See also: Lindzen, Richard S., *Absence of Scientific Basis*, Research & Exploration, A Scholarly Publication of the National Geographic Society, Spring, 1993.

(5) Schneider, Stephen, Discover Magazine, October, 1989.

(6) Time Magazine, April 9, 2001. The cover picture shows a black frying pan with an egg half cooked. The yoke of the egg depicts a globe and shows North America and most of South America. Cover title: Global Warming. Subtitles: Climbing Temperatures. Melting Glaciers. Rising Seas. All over the earth we're feeling the heat. Why isn't Washington?

(7) Hansen, James, *Climate Forcings in the Industrial Era*, Proceedings of the National Academy of Sciences, October 27, 1998.

Appendix—Key Abbreviations, Acronyms and Chemicals

AB—Assembly Bill
AE—Alternative Energy. See also Note (8), Chapter 5.
AEI—American Enterprise Institute
ANWR—Arctic National Wildlife Refuge
AP—Associated Press
ASLS—Aerosols. See also Note (7), Chapter 7.

BC—British Columbia
BANANA—Build Absolutely Nothing, Anytime, Near Anything
BOHICA—Bend Over, Here It Comes Again
BPA—Bonnyville Power Administration
BPD—Barrels per Day

CAFE—Corporate Averag Fuel Economy
CAR2002—Climate Action Report for 2002
CDC—Center for Disease Control
CEI—Competitive Enterprise Institute
CERA—Cambridge Energy Research Associates
CFCs—An abbreviation for chloroflourocarbons, a complex mixture of
    chemicals containing carbon, chlorine, flourine and hydrogen.
CH_4—Chemical formula for methane
CIA—Central Intelligence Agency
COP—Council of the Parties
CO_2—Chemical formula for Carbon Dioxide
CO_2e—Expression for Carbon Dioxide equivalents. A calculated value based
    on the levels of all greenhouse gases in the atmosphere, and their relative
    warming characteristics.
CO—Chemical formula for Carbon Monoxide
CPEX—California Power Exchange
CPUC—California Public Utility Commission
CSE—Citizens for a Sound Economy

EMA—Earth Motion Anomalies
EPA—Environmental Protection Agency

FBI—Federal Bureau of Investigation
FCCC—Framework Convention on Climate Change
FERC—Federal Energy Regulatory Commission

GCM—General Circulation Model
GCMI—George C. Marshall Institute
GHG—Greenhouse Gas. Includes CO_2, CH_4, CFCs, N_2O and stratospheric O_3.
GW—Gigawatt, a basic unit of electrical capacity, a billion watts
gwh—gigawatt hour, a basic unit of electrical energy, a billion watt hours
HG—Head Goron
Hg—Chemical symbol for Mercury

IPCC—Intergovernmental Panel on Climate Change. Reports jointly to UNEP
    and WMO.
ISO—Independent System Operator

JFK—John F. Kennedy
JFK*—John F. Kerry

K—Kilo, a thousand
KP—Kyoto Protocol
KW—Kilowatt, a basic unit of electrical capacity, a thousand watts
kwh—kilowatt hour, a basic unit of electrical energy, a thousand watt hours
KY—Kiloyears
KYBP—Kiloyears before present

LIA—Little IceAge

m—Meter
M—Mega, a million
MBPD—Millions of barrels per day
MIT—Massachusetts Institute of Technology
MW—Megawatt, a basic unit of electrical capacity, a million watts
mwh—megawatt hour, a basic unit of electrical energy, a million watt hours
MWP—Medievil Warming Period

NACC—National Assessment of Future Impacts of Climate Change
NAS—National Academy of Sciences
NASA—National Aeronautics and Space Administration
NCAR—National Center for Atmospheric Research
NGO—Non Governmental Organization
NIMBY—Not In My Back Yard
N_2—Chemical formula for nitrogen
N_2O—Chemical formula for dinitrogen oxide
NO_2—Chemical formula for nitrogen dioxide
NO_x—Chemical expression for a family of nitrogen oxides
NOAA—National Oceanic and Atmospheric Adminisration
NOPE—Not on Planet Earth
NYMEX—New York Mercantile Exchange

O&GJ—Oil & Gas Journal
OPEC—Organization of Petroleum Exporting Countries
O_2—Chemical formula for oxygen
O_3—Chemical formula for ozone

PG&E—Pacific Gas and Electric utility
POW/MIA—Prisoner of War/Missing in Action
ppm—Parts per million
PURPA—Public Utility Regulatory Policy Act

QF—Qualified Facility

SCE—Southern California Edison
SD—Sustainable Deevelopment
SDG&E—San Diego Gas and Electric
SEPP—Science and Environmental Policy Project
SMUD—Sacramento Municipal Utility District
SO_2—Chemical formula for Sulfur Dioxide
SOA—Solar Output Anomaly. Includes sunspots and solar flares. See also Note
   (5), Chapter 4 for more details on sunspots.
SUVs—Sport Utility Vehicles

THC—Thermo-haline circulation
TWTW—The Week That Was, an Internet newsletter, by SEPP

UB—Unabomber
UBC—University of British Columbia
UN or U. N.—United Nations
UNEP—United Nations Environmental Program

VVAW—Vietnam Veterans Against the War

WMO—World Meteorological Organization

ZEVs—Zero Emission Vehicles

0-595-33419-9

www.ingramcontent.com/pod-product-compliance
Lightning Source LLC
Chambersburg PA
CBHW020243290526
45784CB00003B/1092